WHAT CAN THE RIGHTEOUS DO?

COURAGEOUS LIVING IN A GODLESS CULTURE

PAUL CHAPPELL

All Scripture quotations are taken from the King James Version.
Special emphasis in verses is added.

First published in 2024 by Striving Together Publications.

Striving Together Publications
4020 E. Lancaster Blvd.
Lancaster, CA 93535
800.201.7748

Edited by Monica Bass
Cover Design by Tricia Poledna

The author and publication team have put forth every effort to give proper credit to quotes and thoughts that are not original with the author. It is not our intent to claim originality with any quote or thought that could not readily be tied to an original source.

ISBN 978-1-59894-545-4
ISBN (ebook) 978-1-59894-546-1
Printed in the United States of America

CONTENTS

INTRODUCTION

WHAT CAN THE RIGHTEOUS DO?

In a very real sense, walking the streets of Rome is walking through millennia of history. From the Colosseum where Christians were publicly executed for sport, to the stones on the Appian Way over which first-century disciples of Christ carried the message of the gospel, to the Mamertine Prison where Paul was held before his martyrdom, each scene reminds us of the heritage of courage, perseverance, and faith of the earliest Christians.

I had learned about the Great Fire of Rome in 64 AD while in high school, but actually walking the streets of the city where it had blazed gave me a new perspective of its place in history and its terrible significance to the Christians who lived in Rome at the time. For it was this fire that sparked the first great persecution of the early church.

The historian Tacitus, who was in Rome at the time, described the scene:

> ...Now started the most terrible and destructive fire which Rome had ever experienced. It began in the Circus, where it adjoins the Palatine and Caelian hills. Breaking out in shops selling inflammable goods, and fanned by the wind, the conflagration instantly grew and swept the whole length of the Circus. There were no walled mansions or temples, or any other obstructions, which could arrest it. First, the fire swept violently over the level spaces. Then it climbed the hills-but returned to ravage the lower ground again. It outstripped every counter-measure.... Terrified, shrieking women, helpless old and young, people intent on their own safety, people unselfishly supporting invalids or waiting for them, fugitives and lingerers alike–all heightened the confusion.[1]

How the fire was started remains a mystery. But in the days following, Nero was accused by many, and with some probable cause. Whether or not he was responsible is impossible to determine. But that he needed to deflect the blame is certain. And he found his scapegoat in the Christians, which he publicly accused of setting the city on fire.

Tacitus records the awful results:

> In order to drown the rumor, Nero fastened the guilt and inflicted the most exquisite tortures on a class... called

> Christians by the populace.... Covered with the skins of beasts, they were torn by dogs and perished, or were nailed to crosses, or were doomed to the flames and burnt, to serve as a nightly illumination, when daylight had expired. Nero offered his own gardens for this spectacle.[2]

I can only imagine the sense of despair many Christians must have felt. They were, by all accounts, good citizens. Aside from being unwilling to ascribe deity to the Emperor, they were model Romans. Their very religion instructed them to pray for leaders, submit to authority, and seek the peace of their communities. Yet, now they were being falsely accused and tortured for a crime they did not commit. In reality, they were being persecuted for their faith (their identity as Christians was what Nero singled out), but they weren't even given the public benefit of standing for Christ. Rather, they were treated as disloyal citizens and arsonists.

What was a Christian to do?

Something similar, if partially figurative, is happening in the United States today.

A country once strong and majestic, once the beacon of hope for nations around the world, appears to be crumbling. Activists openly admit to bringing in a new world order in which the United States abandons any religious values—

particularly any attached to Christianity—and instead focuses on preferred pronouns, the gender transition of children, and stirring accusations of racism and bigotry.

In some cases, such as during the open riots of 2020, cities literally burned while politicians and city leaders excused the lawless destruction as "mostly peaceful protests." Still today, in Los Angeles County where I pastor, open theft takes place in businesses while the legal system is discouraged from prosecuting it. Every observant, honest citizen knows that our nation's southern border has both drugs and human trafficking flowing across it. All the while, politicians in Washington, D.C., are locked in partisan fighting over ridiculous issues.

These things grieve patriotic citizens. But they are just the fruit of a deeper, more sinister root. Underneath these symptoms, there is a blatant rejection of God and of any objective standard of morality. Consider a few examples that have taken place within months of this writing:

- A young man reading the Bible on the sidewalk outside a Pride and drag queen event was arrested for "public disturbance."[3]
- A Christian mother in Oregon was unable to adopt foster children because she does not believe in "gender affirmation."[4]

- A Major League Baseball team honored a group of gay men who dress as women and perform obscene and vulgar acts at churches and in front of children at the team's pride night game.[5]
- Multiple states, including the state where I pastor, are writing laws to allow children to pursue gender-change surgeries without parental consent.[6]

I don't write this to frighten you. As an American, I hope and pray that the protections woven into the *United States Constitution* somehow withstand this terrible strain. I'm thankful for every flicker of encouragement in grassroots movements or court decisions that reinforce morality and religious liberty—such as the overturning of Roe v. Wade and the Supreme Court's decision in favor of religious liberty in football coach Joe Kennedy's case. I believe our country is worth every sacrifice to preserve liberty.

But I also don't have my head buried in the sand. As I look back over the past several years, the trajectory is clear. Unless there is a sudden change of direction, America is either headed for anarchy or revival. And the result of either will influence the rest of the world. While I pray fervently for revival, I believe Christians need a better strategy than the two I see most often displayed—remaining oblivious or becoming fearful.

It's not hard to imagine that real persecution, like the first-century Christians in Rome experienced, is coming. It's not hard to envision a day when a committed Christian living in the United States of America is oppressed. Even today, as patriotic Christians survey the damage being done to the moral and civil fabric of our nation, many feel they are watching their country burn.

And this isn't happening in America alone. It seems the Western world, including Canada and the United Kingdom, are bent on the dual goals of breaking down the values that strengthen a society and of accusing those who hold to these values (particularly Christians) as being the problem.

So here are the questions of this book: What is a Christian to do? What *can* a Christian do?

You and I are not the first ones to ask what believers can do to stem the tide of evil.

Some three thousand years ago, as the future King, David fled for his life from a deranged King Saul, he also grieved the demise of his nation.

He experienced first-hand what it was to be targeted simply because of faith in God and God's purposes for his life. With an unhinged King Saul on his heels, David observed, "For, lo, the wicked bend their bow, they make ready their arrow upon the string, that they may privily shoot at the upright in heart" (Psalm 11:2).

David knew what it was to see the foundations of his nation that had been built on a covenant relationship with God crumbling. And as he pours out his heart in Psalm 11:3, he records an important question it seems others were posing to him: "If the foundations be destroyed, what can the righteous do?"

This question seems to have been asked in either a taunting (if posed by David's enemies) or fatalistic (if by his friends) way. It could be worded in today's vernacular, "If the foundations are destroyed, what's left to do?" The answer is meant to be clear: "nothing."

But is that really the final answer? What *can* the righteous do? This book seeks to bring hope, clarity, and answers to that question.

1 } STAND ON TRUTH

As the culture changes, Christians must stand firm on God's Word.

It was hard to say which was the most stifling—the summer Philadelphia heat or the bickering and objections each time a suggestion was raised. It was 1787, and the Constitutional Convention had been meeting for over a month but had made little to no progress on forming the American Constitution.

Finally, at the end of another day of heated debate, an elderly member of the convention stood to his feet and arrested the attention of the group. "Mr. President," he began, "the small progress we have made after four or five weeks... and continual reasonings with each other—our different sentiments on almost every question... is methinks a melancholy proof of the imperfection of the Human Understanding."

By this time in American history, the speaker, Benjamin Franklin, was looked to as a true statesman. Everyone listened as he made what is perhaps the most-remembered suggestion from that gathering:

> In this situation of this Assembly groping as it were in the dark to find political truth, and scarce able to distinguish it when presented to us, how has it happened, Sir, that we have not hitherto once thought of humbly applying to the Father of lights to illuminate our understandings?...*I have lived, Sir, a long time and the longer I live, the more convincing proofs I see of this truth—that God governs in the affairs of men. And if a sparrow cannot fall to the ground without his notice, is it probable that an empire can rise without his aid?*...I therefore beg leave to move—that henceforth prayers imploring the assistance of Heaven, and its blessings on our deliberations, be held in this Assembly every morning before we proceed to business.[1]

Benjamin Franklin's call to prayer was a turning point for the Constitutional Convention. Soon, the contentious, rancorous spirit that had marked bitter divisions between delegates softened into a spirit of cooperation and brotherhood. The resulting *United States Constitution* is unparalleled in its excellence.

That Franklin was a born-again Christian seems unlikely. His own testimony, at least a couple of decades before his death, indicated that he was not.[2]

Yet, what is striking about this historical moment in American history is that the prevailing attitude in the nation's founding was a belief in God and an assumption that biblical principles and Christian ethics would make people flourish. And this is not the only incident in which this is obvious. A simple read of founding documents, a glance at the inscriptions on early American buildings in Philadelphia or Washington, D.C., and even the print on our currency reveals a founding trust in God. Researchers at the University of Houston examined fifteen thousand published documents from the men who wrote the *Constitution* and determined that 34 percent of their direct quotes were from the Bible.[3]

Today, however, American leaders and educators who have been influenced by humanistic thought are denying the Christian roots of our nation and seem to be racing one another to get as far from biblical understandings of morality as possible.

For instance, consider that Harvard University was founded in 1636 with the following mission statement: "To be plainly instructed and consider well that the main end of your life and studies is to know God and Jesus Christ." Today, the president of the Harvard Chaplains Organization is Greg Epstein, a self-described atheist whose most popular book is titled *Good Without God.*

There is no doubt that our culture is rapidly moving away from God and from biblical values. It seems that every week there is a new way in which cultural activists push the publicly-accepted boundaries increasingly further from biblical truth.

So what are Christians to do? Give up? Resign themselves to the fact that their children are being actively targeted by ungodly individuals with anti-God ideologies? Go all in on raising political awareness and getting right-leaning politicians elected? Move to the most conservative state they can find and hide?

None of these are long-term solutions. Frankly, they aren't even short-term solutions.

But there is a solution. Yes, our culture is changing, but Christians have an unchanging source of truth. Christians must stand firm on God's Word. They must know what they believe if they and their families are not going to be uprooted by the changing culture.

Understand the Moment

What's happening in America today isn't random. It's not accidental. The very issues that are brought up as moral controversies are a direct attack on the authority of God and the reliability of His Word.

It is *God* who set the sanctity of life when He made man in His own image and set a death penalty for murder of innocent people.

> *So God created man in his own image, in the image of God created he him; male and female created he them. (Genesis 1:27)*

> *Whoso sheddeth man's blood, by man shall his blood be shed: for in the image of God made he man. (Genesis 9:6)*

It is *God* who created civil government and ordained law and order versus anarchy and rebellion.

> *Let every soul be subject unto the higher powers. For there is no power but of God: the powers that be are ordained of God. Whosoever therefore resisteth the power, resisteth the ordinance of God: and they that resist shall receive to themselves damnation. (Romans 13:1–2)*

It is *God* who promised a blessing on those who bless Israel and a curse on those who curse her.

And I will bless them that bless thee, and curse him that curseth thee: and in thee shall all families of the earth be blessed. (Genesis 12:3)

It is *God* who determined that there are two genders.

So God created man in his own image, in the image of God created he him; male and female created he them. (Genesis 1:27)

But from the beginning of the creation God made them male and female. (Mark 10:6)

It is *God* who created marriage and set it as an exclusive, life-long relationship between one man and one woman.

Therefore shall a man leave his father and his mother, and shall cleave unto his wife: and they shall be one flesh. (Genesis 2:24)

For this cause shall a man leave his father and mother, and cleave to his wife; And they twain shall be one flesh: so then they are no more twain, but one flesh. What therefore God hath joined together, let not man put asunder. (Mark 10:7–9)

Yet, any one of those statements are seen today as narrow-minded and, in some cases, immoral.

This is because our culture has lost its moral compass, and instead of accepting biblical truth at face value, it has created its own moral code that exchanges lies for truth. That's what Romans 1:25 describes: "Who changed the truth of God into a lie, and worshipped and served the creature more than the Creator."

This fuller passage describes that people who reject God as the Lawgiver follow a process that leads to redefining human sexuality to fit their distorted desires. We are seeing this play out in our culture today.

> *Because that, when they knew God, they glorified him not as God, neither were thankful; but became vain in their imaginations, and their foolish heart was darkened. Professing themselves to be wise, they became fools,... Wherefore God also gave them up to uncleanness through the lusts of their own hearts, to dishonour their own bodies between themselves: Who changed the truth of God into a lie, and worshipped and served the creature more than the Creator, who is blessed for ever. Amen. For this cause God gave them up unto vile affections: for even their women*

did change the natural use into that which is against nature: (Romans 1:21–22, 24–26)

With these truths in mind, Christians cannot simply bury their heads in the sand and "go along to get along" as the world demands they support increasingly-godless expressions of sexual confusion. They can't just assume that every situation is an isolated incident that comes from a well-meaning but confused person.

Christians must step back and see the larger picture. This is not a "culture war"—merely a clash of the old with the new, of your grandparents' ideas with Gen Z. This is a "truth war"—a direct assault on the authority of God Himself.

Seen in this light, the responsibility of Christians is clear. We must make a determination to stand for God and for truth. How do we do that?

Trust in God's Word

In the midst of the moral confusion of our day, God's Word stands true. It shines as a light in the darkness—revealing God, His love for mankind, the sin that separates us from God, the atoning work of Christ that can reconcile man to God, and the life of holiness that God has designed for us to live.

In fact, the Word of God is the *only* inerrant source of truth and the absolute rule by which we can determine right and wrong.

Think about the incredible nature of God's Word.

It was directly inspired by God. He breathed every word of Scripture: "All scripture is given by inspiration of God…" (2 Timothy 3:16). "For the prophecy came not in old time by the will of man: but holy men of God spake as they were moved by the Holy Ghost" (2 Peter 1:21).

Amazingly, God used more than forty different men from a variety of backgrounds over a time span of 1,500 years to record each word. The writing took place on three contents (Europe, Asia, and Africa) and in three languages (Hebrew, Aramaic, and Greek). Yet, the entire book completely agrees and has been validated time and again by history, archaeology, and science.

If you asked ten contemporary authors to individually write their viewpoint on just one controversial subject, you would come up with a wide range of conflicting opinions. And yet, the Bible covers hundreds of controversial subjects by many different writers—and the entire book agrees. There can be only one reason for this: the Bible has just one Author—God.

And this very Word of God is preserved for us today. "The grass withereth, the flower fadeth: but the word of our God shall stand for ever" (Isaiah 40:8).

Do you realize what that means? You and I can hold in our hands the actual preserved Word of God—His revelation to us. God's Word is objective truth in a changing world. It is pure and right in a day of darkness and confusion. "Every word of God is pure: he is a shield unto them that put their trust in him" (Proverbs 30:5).

These basic truths about God's Word are Christian doctrine 101. So why am I reiterating them here? Because our world is bent on casting doubt on God's Word, claiming it is outdated and irrelevant. The world paints Scripture as harsh and Bible-believing Christians as bigots. Even "progressive Christians" go along with these views as they explain away the Bible as a mere human book, allowing them to pick and choose which passages they will accept.

If you are going to stand for Christ in a God-rejecting culture, you will need an unshakable conviction in the accuracy, authority, and relevance of God's Word to your beliefs and daily life.

A real trust in God's Word goes beyond a theoretical ascent that the Bible is true, to a heart-level belief that God is *right.* It is a trust that God's wisdom as revealed in His Word is good and righteous and the best way for people to live.

Let's bring this distinction down to the real world. If a classmate or co-worker poses a question like, "Why does God hate gays?" or "But do you really think that a boy who feels trapped in a girl's body should be forced to live as someone he is not?" do you cringe? Do you feel like you have to explain away the clear truths of Scripture and avoid questions about the moral laws God has written into human life? Or do you believe that God's way is the *best* way—including for the person actually experiencing same-sex attraction or gender confusion?

These questions get to the heart of if we merely believe God's Word in an academic, doctrinal sense—"Of course I believe the Bible!"—or if we believe that God's Word is the good and perfect revelation of His wisdom for humanity to flourish.

The wisdom of God is expressed through His Word. In Psalm 33:10–11, the Bible gives us a contrast of worldly wisdom and God's wisdom: "The LORD bringeth the counsel of the heathen to nought: he maketh the devices of the people of none effect. The counsel of the LORD standeth for ever, the thoughts of his heart to all generations."

God brings human counsel to *nought*—to nothing. People who think they know what is best for them better than God knows what is best for them will find that He knew their plans and brought them to the emptiness they started with. Romans 1:26–27 gives us a fuller picture of how this takes place: "For this cause God gave them up unto vile affections: for even their women did change the natural use into that which is against nature: And likewise also the men, leaving the natural use of the woman, burned in their lust one toward another; men with men working that which is unseemly, and receiving in themselves that recompence of their error which was meet."

God allows people to reject Him, but the consequence is that they experience the pain of their chosen ways. Meanwhile, God gives His people the truth of His Word and calls us to share with others how they can have a life-changing relationship with Jesus Christ.

Beware of Accommodating Theology

One of the sad commentaries on the apostasy of our day is that people who claim the name of Christ are among the more vocal supporters of the godless agendas of the day. Even *churches* have spurned Scripture as the absolute Word of God. As I travel the nation, I see churches with pride flags out front and messages on their signs supporting everything from gay marriage to transgenderism to Critical Race Theory to Marxism...everything except Jesus Christ and His gospel. Entire denominations have abandoned any pretense of submission to Scripture as their final rule of faith and practice, instead serving as centers to regurgitate the prevailing cultural messages with "Love your neighbor" wording thrown in to Christianize their message.

Some of this is simply evidence of the apostasy that the Bible warned us will come. It is the great "falling away" of 2 Thessalonians 2:3 and of the people who "shall turn away their ears from the truth, and shall be turned unto fables" of 2 Timothy 4:4. No doubt, some of the people and churches who deny or refuse to declare what the Bible actually teaches on these topics of the day never were born-again believers or preachers of the gospel of Christ's death, burial, and resurrection for our sin.

But the challenge for Bible-believing Christians is that we must not follow the example of liberal, woke Christianity. As our culture turns to wickedness, Christians must not abandon biblical convictions; they must study them out in Scripture.

Know What Scripture Teaches

So how about you? Do you know what the Bible teaches about the doctrines that form your faith and Christian practice?

- The inspiration and authority of Scripture
- The deity of Christ
- The way of salvation through Christ
- The New Testament local church
- Creation and the sanctity of human life
- Gender as the creation of God
- The institution of marriage and the biblical family
- The holiness of the Christian life
- The sufficiency of Scripture for all matters pertaining to life and godliness

This list is just a starter. And the point is not to discourage you if you haven't studied these biblically. It is, rather, to encourage you with the fact that the Bible speaks clearly to every one of these issues.

If you don't know what you believe from Scripture, you will be susceptible to faulty theology that undermines biblical truth. Once that happens, it's only a matter of time until you no longer have the truth.

Repeating what other people have told you is not enough. You need to know the biblical reason behind what you believe. You need to know what the Bible teaches on the vital topics of our day.

So what can you do? The answer is simple: study Scripture. Paul exhorted Timothy in 2 Timothy 2:15, "Study to shew thyself approved unto God, a workman that needeth not to be ashamed, rightly dividing the word of truth."

Don't let the word *study* conjure up negative thoughts of reading a dry textbook or cramming for a test. For one thing, God's Word is interesting and relevant, and it is applicable to our daily lives. It's worth our focused attention and intense study. But even so, not all study of Scripture need be intense or technical. There are multiple ways we learn from God's Word. Here are a few of the core ways:

- ***Read Scripture daily.*** There is no substitute in the Christian life for the regular intake of God's Word. Job said, "I have esteemed the words of his mouth more than my necessary food" (Job 23:12). Just as we eat daily, so we should daily nourish our souls in God's Word. Reading through the New Testament or the entire Bible in a year can be a great way to become grounded in the larger truths of Scripture.

- ***Attend church faithfully.*** The pastor's job is to preach God's Word (2 Timothy 4:2). So if you are in a Bible-preaching church, you should be hearing God's Word expounded. There is an accumulation of spiritual understanding that takes place as you sit under biblical preaching from week to week. Additionally, most churches have small groups that meet weekly. These groups are essentially Bible study groups. Those are tremendous opportunities to build weekly Bible study into your life.
- ***Study a topic about which you have questions.*** What are the areas about which you personally have questions? Or what are the areas, perhaps even from the list above, that you have a general sense of what the Bible may teach on this issue, but you couldn't articulate it from the Bible to someone else? Those are a great place to start on a topical Bible study. Ask your pastor or another mature Christian what key passages relate to a given topic and begin right there. Read those passages, and make notes on what they teach. Ask follow up questions. As you repeat this process, you'll understand what the Bible teaches about these matters of importance.

- ***Apply Scripture.*** One of the ways we discover the sufficiency of Scripture is by applying it to our daily lives and to cultural questions. As you encounter questions or decisions, train yourself to ask, "What does the Bible say about this?" The Bible is not only "given by inspiration of God," but it "is *profitable* for doctrine, for reproof, for correction, for instruction in righteousness" (2 Timothy 3:16). It guides and directs us in every significant area of life.
- ***Share Scripture with others.*** If you want to learn something well, commit to teaching it to others. That decision alone prompts study. After all, the teacher always learns more than the student, because of the study the teacher invests. How do we share Scripture with others? All of us should be sharing the essential truth of salvation by faith in Jesus alone with people who don't know Christ (Mark 16:15). If you're a parent, you have been given direct instruction to teach your children God's Word (Deuteronomy 6:7). There are a hundred ways to do this, including short family devotions, talking about the Lord and His Word throughout the day, and helping them evaluate issues or decisions biblically. As Christians, we should also be investing

in teaching younger Christians (2 Timothy 2:2). You might do this through a formal discipleship program, coming alongside to encourage someone in their faith, or perhaps teaching in a children's ministry or small group at church. In any case, as you prepare to share Scripture, you'll be strengthened through your own study.

The great British statesman William Wilberforce said, "There are four things that we ought to do with the Word of God—admit it as the Word of God, commit it to our hearts and minds, submit to it, and transmit it to the world."[4] Are you engaged in these activities?

Stand on Biblical Convictions

At the end of the day, a stand for truth will require courage. It will require Christians with biblical convictions that run deeper than the allure of being accepted or avoiding persecution that may come from their stand.

And that stand is worth it. The men and women who have changed the world have been the men and women the world could not change. Of course, this hasn't stopped the world from trying. Long is the list of Christians who have been threatened—and some martyred—for their stand for truth and for God.

From Elijah to Daniel to John the Baptist to the apostle Paul, those in the pages of Scripture who made a difference were those who stood firm in their faith even when the whole world was against them.

History, too, records the lives of men and women such as John Huss, Anne Askew, William Tyndale, Hugh Latimer, John Bunyan, and many others who held to the truth and lifted up the gospel when it would have saved their lives and freedom to not take a stand. But their courageous stands preserved the truth for us today.

And that is what our decision to stand will do for those who come after us. May God enable you and me to be among the men and women today who determine to stand on truth.

2} PRAY FOR REVIVAL

Some battles will only be won through prayer.

Nestled in the biography section of my study library is a slim, 140-page hardback volume titled *How I Know God Answers Prayer.* This little book was written by missionary Rosalind Goforth and was published in 1921. It is a record of personal testimonies to answered prayers in her life and her husband Jonathan's life as they served in China.

Reading page after page of one woman's reliance on God through prayer is both encouraging and convicting. It's encouraging to be reminded that God *does* answer prayer. And it's convicting to consider the cost of neglected prayer. James 4:2 tells us, ". . .ye have not, because ye ask not."

One of the stories in this book ends in a phrase that has always challenged me. Rosalind relates how her husband was attempting to begin a church plant in the northern part of China's Hunan province. This province is regarded as one of the cradles of Chinese civilization, and the Goforths found it extremely resistant to the entrance of foreigners. No one wanted to rent to them, much less to listen to their message of the gospel. Once they did find a place to begin, their premises were physically assaulted and vandalized.

As the difficulties in front of them sank in, the Goforths received a letter from missionary Hudson Taylor, founder of the China Inland Mission. He wrote, "We understand North Hunan is to be your field; we, as a mission, have tried for ten years to enter that province from the south, and have only just succeeded. It is one of the most anti-foreign provinces in China. . . . *Brother, if you would enter that province, you must go forward on your knees.*"[1]

That instruction—"you must go forward on your knees"—is good advice for every Christian.

This Is War

The challenges facing Christians today are larger than can be solved with political strategy or human energy. The need before us is greater than can be met by planning, preparation, and diligent work. Spiritual needs require spiritual solutions. And the needs in front of us are spiritual.

The decay of America, or of any other culture for that matter, is not merely a war of conflicting ideals or viewpoints. It is a nation actively rejecting God.

The answer then is not simply to persuade a large number of people to change their minds. It is to pray for the moving of God on the hearts of people.

I think of Paul writing the epistle of Ephesians from prison in Rome. As he reminded the Ephesian church of the riches that were theirs in Christ (chapters 1–3) and of the importance of walking as a child of God in every facet of life (chapters 4–6), he concluded by challenging them that they were in a spiritual battle. This is the context of the well-known passage on the armor of God.

> *Finally, my brethren, be strong in the Lord, and in the power of his might. Put on the whole armour of God, that ye may be able to stand against the wiles of the devil. For we wrestle not against flesh and blood, but against principalities, against powers, against the rulers of the darkness of this world, against spiritual wickedness in high places. Wherefore take unto you the whole armour of God, that ye may be able to withstand in the evil day, and having done all, to stand. Stand therefore, having your loins girt about with truth, and having on the breastplate of righteousness; And your*

> *feet shod with the preparation of the gospel of peace; Above all, taking the shield of faith, wherewith ye shall be able to quench all the fiery darts of the wicked. And take the helmet of salvation, and the sword of the Spirit, which is the word of God: (Ephesians 6:10–17)*

But think for a moment with me about the climax of this passage. Directly following the verses with which we are so familiar is a call to *pray.*

> ***Praying always with all prayer and supplication in the Spirit,*** *and watching thereunto with all perseverance and supplication for all saints; And for me, that utterance may be given unto me, that I may open my mouth boldly, to make known the mystery of the gospel, (Ephesians 6:18–19)*

Paul knew that spiritual battles must be fought with spiritual weapons. He not only challenged the Ephesian believers to pray, but he requested they pray for *him.* We can conclude from this passage that Paul believed prayer to be a powerful and needful element of spiritual warfare.

So, how should we pray in light of the needs of our nation and our own desire to make a difference?

Pray in Confession

Two of the great men of prayer in the Old Testament were Daniel and Nehemiah. Both men served God in times of national spiritual decay. Both men were godly leaders. But remarkably, both prayed prayers of confession.

> *And I prayed unto the Lord my God, and made my confession, and said, O Lord, the great and dreadful God, keeping the covenant and mercy to them that love him, and to them that keep his commandments; We have sinned, and have committed iniquity, and have done wickedly, and have rebelled, even by departing from thy precepts and from thy judgments:* (Daniel 9:4–5)

> *Let thine ear now be attentive, and thine eyes open, that thou mayest hear the prayer of thy servant, which I pray before thee now, day and night, for the children of Israel thy servants, and confess the sins of the children of Israel, which we have sinned against thee: both I and my father's house have sinned.* (Nehemiah 1:6)

It's easy for us to point to the need "out there" without taking seriously the need "in here"—the need of our own hearts.

I heard about a man who responded to the invitation at an evangelistic service. "I am a Christian," he told the counselor who met him at the front altar, "but there is a sin in my life, and I need help." The counselor read some verses of Scripture and then encouraged him to confess his sins to God. The man began to pray, "Oh Father, if we have done anything wrong. . . ." The counselor interrupted him. "Don't drag me into your sin! There is no *if* or *we* involved. If you want forgiveness, you need to get down to business with God!"

Every honest Christian knows that he sins daily. In thought, word, action, or habit, in sins of commission, and in sins of omission, we each sin. But how long has it been since you sincerely asked the Lord to search your heart and reveal your sin to you that you might specifically confess it to Him?

> *Search me, O God, and know my heart: try me, and know my thoughts: And see if there be any wicked way in me, and lead me in the way everlasting. (Psalm 139:23–24)*

It is through this process of humbling ourselves before the Lord that we receive God's grace and draw near to Him.

> *But he giveth more grace. Wherefore he saith, God resisteth the proud, but giveth grace unto the humble. Submit yourselves therefore to God. Resist the devil, and he will flee from you. Draw nigh to God, and he will draw nigh to you. Cleanse your hands, ye sinners; and purify your hearts, ye double minded. (James 4:6–8)*

We cannot pray for revival in our nation if we do not have revival in our own hearts.

Pray for Revival

Several years ago, Terrie and I had the opportunity to visit Wales. I was especially interested in seeing the places where the Welsh Revival of 1904–05 had broken out. As we toured the village of Rhos, a center for that revival, we saw churches on nearly every corner. We decided to walk down a street and ask locals we saw what they knew about the revival.

The Welsh people are kind. Many were outside and happy to talk with the American tourists about their town. But most had never even heard of that revival. Finally, we met an elderly lady who lit up when we asked about the Welsh Revival. She shared with us that her mother was saved during the revival under the preaching of Evan

Roberts. She also was also a Christian who loved the Lord and wished more people in her town knew Him and knew their amazing spiritual heritage of the revival that had birthed in their town.

Her grandmother's salvation was a turning point so that one hundred years and four or five generations later, members of this family loved the Lord and were faithful in church.

As Terrie and I left Rhos, we had a renewed realization of the need for revival in every generation. God worked mightily through the Great Welsh Revival in the early 1900s. But most of the people living there today don't even know that it happened, much less experience the benefits of it.

Similarly, God has blessed America with past revivals. In the earliest years of our nation, the First Great Awakening (1730s–40s) swept through the colonies under the preaching of Jonathan Edwards and George Whitfield.

In the time following the American Revolution, our nation was in spiritual decline. One of the several contributing factors was Thomas Paine's *The Age of Reason,* which sought to debunk biblical Christianity and gained great popularity in American colleges. But in 1794, a group of Baptist pastors drafted a circular letter to churches of every denomination asking their members to dedicate days in prayer for revival in America. By the end of 1795, the Second Great Awakening had begun and continued for *fifty* years. God's people drew close to the Savior, and whole towns were converted to Christ.

America today needs another revival—another widespread awakening of people who realize their guilt before God and their need for salvation.

Do you pray for God to bring this revival? Do you cry out with the psalmist, "Wilt thou not revive us again: that thy people may rejoice in thee?" (Psalm 85:6).

Some Christians think that the rejection of God in America is too pronounced, too deliberate, for God to send another revival. But there has never been a revival anywhere in human history—Wales, the United States, or anywhere else—that was not preceded by a turning *away* from God. For without spiritual decay, there is no need for revival. Thus, there is hope for *any* nation through a turning to God. We don't look to the government or society at large for change; we ask God to revive His church and convict the lost.

Revival doesn't start "out there"—it starts within the church. If churches across America were shaken with a fervor and intense desire to see God work, our culture would be impacted.

As bad as the situation seems to be today, there is still a solution available. God made a wonderful promise to Solomon at the dedication of the temple. Though it was primarily intended for the people of Israel, the principle is applicable to us today. "If my people, which are called by my name, shall humble themselves, and pray, and seek my face, and turn from their wicked ways; then will I hear from heaven, and will forgive their sin, and will heal their land" (2 Chronicles 7:14).

I believe that God is fully in control, but He also calls us to be fully engaged—in prayer. "...The effectual fervent prayer of a righteous man availeth much" (James 5:16).

Pray for Leaders

There is no doubt that in God's plan, the local church is to be the catalyst for change in a nation. We do not look to Washington, D.C., for revival; we look to God.

Yet, it is just as indisputable that the actions of government leaders do affect Christians and they do influence the American people—both through their examples and legislation.

Thus, when we pray for revival, we should also pray for our national leaders. We should seek to minister to their needs, encourage any attempts they make toward upholding biblical values, and pray for them to have wisdom to make choices that will preserve the peace of our nation.

In fact, we are biblically commanded to pray for our leaders:

> *I exhort therefore, that, first of all, supplications, prayers, intercessions, and giving of thanks, be made for all men; For kings, and for all that are in authority; that we may lead a quiet and peaceable life in all godliness and honesty. (1 Timothy 2:1–2)*

Paul penned these words of instruction to Timothy when Nero ruled with an iron fist and Christians experienced dire persecution. I'm sure that given the chance, Paul would have voted for a different ruler than Nero. But that didn't stop him from praying for the ruler God allowed.

Regardless of who our elected officials are and of what views they espouse, we should regularly pray for them by name. Pray for their salvation (if they are not Christians), and pray for God to give them wisdom or to intervene in their decisions that we might have the peace and protection to share the gospel in our communities.

Pray for Boldness

Throughout the New Testament, we see the apostles praying for boldness in sharing the message of the gospel. This was the main thrust of Paul's request for personal prayer that we saw a moment ago in Ephesians 6:

> *And for me, that utterance may be given unto me, that I may open my mouth boldly, to make known the mystery of the gospel, (Ephesians 6:19)*

After being threatened by the Jewish leaders to cease and desist preaching the gospel, Peter and John prayed for boldness:

> *And now, Lord, behold their threatenings: and grant unto thy servants, that with all boldness they may speak thy word, (Acts 4:29)*

God answered Peter and John's prayer so that when they finished praying, not only were *they* filled with boldness to speak of Christ, but others were as well.

> *And when they had prayed, the place was shaken where they were assembled together; and they were all filled with the Holy Ghost, and they spake the word of God with boldness. (Acts 4:31)*

If we long for our land to experience revival, there must be men and women who boldly share the gospel with those who don't know Christ.

Is Prayer Enough?

If you believe that Christians cannot expect change in America by prayer alone, you are correct. We can't expect to closet ourselves in prayer and never share the gospel or take a stand on truth or do any of the other actions we'll look at in the coming pages—actions in which Christ commands us to engage—and expect that the needs of our nation will miraculously evaporate. So yes, there is much to be done besides prayer.

But we also must recognize that any of those actions taken *without* prayer will be powerless. E. M. Bounds, a chaplain during the Civil War, wrote in his book *Power through Prayer:*

> What the church needs today is not more machinery or better, not new organizations or more and novel methods, but men who the Holy Spirit can use—men of prayer, men mighty in prayer. The Holy Spirit does not come on machinery but on men. He does not anoint plans, but men—men of prayer.[2]

So is prayer everything? No. But can we expect to move any further than we go on our knees? Also no. As John Bunyan said, "You can do more than pray after you have prayed, but you cannot do more than pray until you have prayed."

3} DECLARE THE GOSPEL

Our world's greatest need is the gospel of Jesus Christ.

The collapse of the French defenses and the rapid advance of the Nazi armies in May of 1940 left hundreds of thousands of British, Canadian, and French forces in danger of being surrounded and destroyed. Operation Dynamo—a desperate rescue effort—was put in place. British officials hoped to save at least 45,000 troops by using naval boats and fishing vessels to ferry them across the English Channel before the Germans arrived. The operation was a huge success, and in the end, nearly 350,000 Allied soldiers were rescued. For a rescue operation, it was hugely successful.

But when Winston Churchill saw that people in England were viewing this as a triumph, he took to the floor of the

House of Commons to point out a painful truth amid the rejoicing: "We must be very careful not to assign to this deliverance the attributes of a victory. Wars are not won by evacuations."[1]

I'm afraid that too many Christians and even churches in America today have the idea that as long as they can hang on to their faith, keep their heads down, and not attract the attention of cancel culture, they have succeeded. But "hanging on" is not what Christ gave us to do. He gave us one mission: "Go ye into all the world, and preach the gospel to every creature" (Mark 16:15).

Now is not the time to retreat; it is the time to press forward for Christ and for lost souls.

The Darker the Night, the Brighter the Light

One of my favorite verses—actually, my life verse—is Romans 1:16: "For I am not ashamed of the gospel of Christ: for it is the power of God unto salvation to every one that believeth; to the Jew first, and also to the Greek."

There is no question that the apostle Paul, who penned those words, had a great burden for the city of Rome. By Paul's day, the city had grown to a population of over one million people. It attracted people from across the empire and is estimated to have had over 420 temples. The Pantheon itself housed all of the gods and goddesses of the Romans, as well as all the gods of the conquered peoples of Rome.

Yet Paul knew that neither the idols nor the sophistication of Rome could save people from their sins.

In fact, it is just a few verses after the one quoted above that Paul describes the downward progression and perversion of people who reject God.

Yet, in the same chapter where Paul defined the godless, pagan lifestyles of the Gentile world, he said, "I am debtor both to the Greeks, and to the Barbarians; both to the wise, and to the unwise. So, as much as in me is, I am ready to preach the gospel to you that are at Rome also" (Romans 1:14–15).

Paul recognized the perverse culture that surrounded him, but he wasn't wringing his hands about it. He didn't assume it was past hope or that nobody wanted to hear or respond to his message. As he looked at the various groups and subcultures around him, instead of withdrawing as a monk or a hermit, he intensified his commitment to preach the gospel.

There is no human society so depraved or so wicked that it is immune to the gospel. The people in our nation today—including those who live in or promote ungodly, immoral lifestyles—are not our enemies; they are our mission field.

In a day of terrible spiritual darkness, there must be Christians and local churches who will rise up and boldly, compassionately, and diligently declare the single truth that people steeped in sin need to hear—the death, burial, and resurrection of Christ for our sins.

Paul instructed the church at Philippi, "That ye may be blameless and harmless, the sons of God, without rebuke, *in the midst of a crooked and perverse nation,* among whom ye shine as lights in the world; Holding forth the word of life…" (Philippians 2:15–16). If there was ever a "crooked and perverse nation," it was the Roman Empire. Sadly, America today is following the same downward path to her own destruction. But rather than taking this as a reason to *hide* the light of the gospel, we must hold forth the word of life. In the deepening darkness, it will shine all the brighter.

Rather than being discouraged and hunkering down to ride out the storm, the most needful response is to do more than ever to reach people with the gospel.

Shameless

Think for a moment of Paul's statement "I am not ashamed of the gospel of Christ" in light of the "shameless" causes of our day. From Pride parades to abortion marches to violent protests in the streets, people publicly and vulgarly celebrate acts of defiance toward God. Things that would have shocked the conscience of most Americans even just a few decades ago are proudly paraded today.

The world champions causes of which it ought to be ashamed while at the same time putting down Christians who lift up the gospel. So far, this pressure is not physical persecution but the shaming of "cancel culture." A Christian who states simple beliefs such as that the Bible is objectively true, God's direct commands provide the standard for sin and guilt before God, Jesus is the only way to Heaven, and human flourishing is furthered when a society follows the moral principles of God's Word face the risk of being silenced, shunned, or publicly humiliated over their "hate speech."

It is in this light that the apostle Paul's boldness in declaring "I am not ashamed of the gospel of Christ" is important for us to remember. Paul was not ashamed to boldly proclaim the supremacy of the gospel over Roman paganism, Greek intellectualism, and Jewish unbelief. "For the Jews require a sign, and the Greeks seek after wisdom: But we preach Christ crucified…" (1 Corinthians 1:22–23).

Paul was regularly mocked or physically assaulted for the message he preached, but he shared it anyway, because he knew that the gospel could change lives.

There is a lot of messaging in our world today. Some of it is helpful, and some of it is not. But there is one message that every Christian must share—that Jesus Christ came into the world to save sinners and offers salvation for all who will call upon Him.

The success of this message is not dependent on American politics or even on religious freedom. It is entirely dependent upon the work of the Holy Spirit and the obedience of Christians. Even when earthly rulers physically persecute God's people and try to thwart the work of God, they cannot. As Paul said, "I suffer trouble, as an evil doer, even unto bonds; but the word of God is not bound" (2 Timothy 2:9).

Personally Share the Gospel

A missionary to Africa told the story of an elderly woman who was reached with the gospel. Though she was blind and could neither read nor write, she wanted to share her newfound faith with others. She went to the missionary and asked him for a copy of the Bible. When she got it, she asked him to underline John 3:16 in red and add a bookmark to the page so she could find it.

The missionary wanted to see how this blind woman planned to use the Bible he marked for her, so one day he followed her. In the afternoon, just before school let out, she made her way to the front door. As the boys came out when school was dismissed, she would stop one and ask if he knew how to read. When he said "Yes" she would ask him to read the verse that was marked in red. Then she would ask, "Do you know what this means?" and she would proceed to tell him about Christ.

The missionary said that when he left the field years later there were twenty-four men pastoring churches who had been led to the Lord when they were school boys by that illiterate blind woman.[2]

It's easy for us to say, "Yes, our world certainly needs the gospel" and then follow with excuses why we cannot personally share it. But God's plan for reaching the world is that each of us who have received His gift of salvation would share the Good News with others. Telling others how to be saved is not meant to be reserved for pastors; it is a command for every Christian. And it does not require brilliant knowledge, gifted speech, or a charming personality; it simply requires obedience.

> *For the preaching of the cross is to them that perish foolishness; but unto us which are saved it is the power of God.... For ye see your calling, brethren, how that not many wise men after the flesh, not many*

> *mighty, not many noble, are called: But God hath chosen the foolish things of the world to confound the wise; and God hath chosen the weak things of the world to confound the things which are mighty;* (1 Corinthians 1:18, 26–27)

What can you do to personally share the gospel? Here are a few suggestions:

- Pray by name for the salvation of those in your life who don't know Christ (family, neighbors, etc.), and then plan a moment to speak to them about Christ.
- Pray daily for Christ's compassion for those who don't know Him and for boldness and opportunity to share the gospel.
- Pick up gospel tracts from your church, carry them with you, and begin offering them to people with whom you interact.
- Schedule time to seek out opportunities to share the gospel—perhaps going door-to-door on the streets of your city to invite people to your church and, more importantly, to a personal relationship with God and a home in Heaven.
- If you are unsure of how to explain the gospel to someone, ask a Christian who is an effective witness to teach you how to lead someone to Christ.[3]

Faithfulness Counts

One of the most effective witnesses I have ever known was a woman whose name most of the world will never know, let alone remember. Her name was Maxine Chappell, and she was my mother.

Mom was a soulwinner like no one else I know. Over the years, she led hundreds of people to Christ—including my mother-in-law. I first learned to share the gospel by going door-to-door soulwinning with my mom when I was eight years old.

The church that I grew up in sent buses into our community to pick up children whose parents didn't bring them to church, much like the church I pastor still does today. Typically, these children came from challenging homes and crime-filled neighborhoods. But that didn't stop my mom. She led one of the bus routes and enlisted me as her "assistant captain"—a title I took seriously. Every Sunday, our route needed not one but two buses because of all the kids and single moms that my mom had reached out to, shared the gospel with, and led to Christ.

I'll never forget an experience I had with Mom a few years ago. She had been dealing with Alzheimer's for some time, and it was taking its toll. She no longer remembered her family or understood her surroundings. I was visiting my parents in Phoenix and took them to In-N-Out Burger. I got up to fill my drink, and before I returned to our booth, I saw my mom passing out gospel tracts to others in the restaurant. With every tract she handed out, she asked, "Do you know for sure that Heaven is your home?" Her memory was fading, but her passion for souls was strong and her habit to share the gospel remained.

You may not lead hundreds of school boys in Africa to Christ. You may not start a city-wide revival or see thousands of people saved. But you can personally and faithfully share the gospel with people who do not know Christ. After all, it is the gospel—not you or me—that is "the power of God unto salvation." Our job is to faithfully share it. *This* is what the righteous can do.

> *To wit, that God was in Christ, reconciling the world unto himself, not imputing their trespasses unto them; and hath committed unto us the word of reconciliation. Now then we are ambassadors for Christ . . . (2 Corinthians 5:19–20)*

4} COMMIT TO THE LOCAL CHURCH

While political movements have their place, the real work of God takes place through the local church.

When the Covid pandemic of 2020 started, none of us had a reference point for how it would progress. But from the earliest days, I had two thoughts in mind as a pastor: obedience to Christ and the safety of our members. Like most churches, ours pivoted to online-only services for a few weeks.

Soon, however, it became apparent that the "fourteen days to slow the spread" slogan was never intended to be taken literally. As the government began to force restrictions on churches while at the same time lifting restrictions from bars and casinos, we determined it was time to chart a safe path to return to in-person services. As a church with several thousand members, this required a multi-service plan that accounted for space for social distancing and time to sanitize facilities between each service. We took every precaution we could to mitigate risk and to assure members. Meanwhile, every Sunday for the next six months, our county sent representatives from the health department to show up at our services to write a citation and issue a fine.

During these challenging days, I remember planning to host a "Comeback Sunday" when the pandemic was over, the cloud was lifted, and all of our church members felt no fear in returning.

What actually took place, however, was different than I anticipated. Although many of our members returned quickly, others had greater health concerns and trickled in over time. But to this day what grieves my heart is that some people—including families who were faithful to every service before the pandemic—never returned. To be sure, many of these returned to work, and their kids returned to school and extracurricular activities, and occasionally I'll see them around town. But they just never quite made it back to church, at least not with the consistency they had before. It was as if Satan used the messaging of Covid and the disruption of their routines to suggest to their hearts that the local church is not essential.

In reality, the local church is one of the few essentials to the Christian life. And commitment to it is one of the greatest decisions a Christian can make—especially in uncertain times.

The Local Church Is Enduring

The Temple of Artemis (also known as the Temple of Diana) at Ephesus was one of the seven wonders of the ancient world. The massive structure, measuring more than 400 feet long and 250 feet wide, was supported by 120 huge marble columns rising 60 feet into the air to support its great weight.

One can't help but think Paul had this building in mind when he wrote to the young pastor Timothy in Ephesus that the "church of the living God" is "the pillar and ground of the truth" (1 Timothy 3:15).

There is an implied contrast there that the Temple of Diana, grand and imposing as it may have seemed to Timothy, was empty inside—a temporary building for a false god. But the church of the *living* God—which is not a building at all but a body of believers—is the true pillar and ground of the truth and will endure forever.

If you visit the site of ancient Ephesus today, all you will find from the Temple of Diana is ruins with a single column, and that stacked from nearby fragments, rising to the sky.

Human movements—religious or political—come and go. But the real work of God on Earth takes place through the local church. From Lancaster, California, to Beijing, China, to Tehran, Iran, you can visit local churches today that are thriving. Of course, in Beijing and Tehran, these churches are "underground." They meet in hidden locations, sometimes changing from week-to-week to avoid unwanted attention by the government. But with or without a building, the local church remains the "pillar and ground of the truth." It is to be both counter-cultural and Christ-exalting.

I'm thankful for political movements that have positively contributed to human flourishing. Every American should thank God for the signers of the *Declaration of Independence* who pledged their "lives, fortunes, and sacred honor" to the cause of freedom. I'm a grateful beneficiary of the sacrifices of those early patriots, as well as the many who have sacrificed in untold ways since then.

But while political movements have their place, they will only be temporary. The real work of God on Earth takes place through the local church. Jesus told Peter, "I will build my church; and the gates of Hell shall not prevail against it" (Matthew 16:18). Jesus made that promise nearly two thousand years ago, and the gates of hell have not prevailed against the church. It has withstood persecution of the fiercest degrees. Yet, the local church remains.

I urge you then, don't anchor your hope to a conservative movement or give your all to a political cause or leader. Do all you can for your country and to preserve freedom, but aside from your family, the only institution that is worthy of your full commitment is the local church.

The Local Church Is Transformational

A few months ago, I met with some of the leaders in our city to discuss city development. As I shared with them some of the aspects that were impacting our church family, one of the men seated at the table spoke up: "Pastor Chappell, Lancaster Baptist Church is the jewel of this city, and we want to do what we can to help—for the sake of the community."

I've thought a lot about what this gentleman said. Since my earliest days as a pastor here, it has been my prayer that no honest history of the Antelope Valley where our church is located could be written without describing the impact of Lancaster Baptist Church. And one of the blessings of serving as a pastor in the same church for nearly forty years is getting to see the impact a gospel-preaching church can have on a community over time. Fundamentally, the gospel changes individual lives. But when many individuals within the same city experience this life change, there is bound to be an effect on the larger community.

There is much that committed Christians can do for their communities. They can serve the homeless, help with community projects, be a friendly neighbor, report crime, etc. But there is nothing more impactful than reaching their community with the gospel. And this best takes place through the local church. After all, it is the local church (comprised at that time of its earliest core of the disciples) that was tasked by Christ with the Great Commission: "Go ye therefore, and teach all nations, baptizing them in the name of the Father, and of the Son, and of the Holy Ghost: Teaching them to observe all things whatsoever I have commanded you: and, lo, I am with you alway, even unto the end of the world. Amen" (Matthew 28:19–20).

I don't mean to indicate that our city is now Christian because of the presence of Lancaster Baptist Church. Although our community is a wonderful place to live, it has the same problems your community has. There is crime, there is homelessness, there is graffiti, and there are drugs. I'm glad for every city program to address needs in our community. But the only real, transformational, life-changing help that broken, hurting people will receive will come through salvation. And God's plan for them to hear the gospel is through an active, obedient, local church.

The Local Church Is Essential

Six years before the Covid pandemic of 2020, the idea of *essentialism* became popular through a best-selling book by that title. *Essentialism: The Disciplined Pursuit of Less* by Greg McKeown urges readers to accomplish more by paring their choices and commitments down to the few that really matter. This is a healthy exercise in nearly every area of our lives. Sometimes we get committed in so many directions that we become distracted by all of them rather than purposeful in any of them.

But by whatever metric you choose to measure the essential value of the local church, it qualifies. The local church is absolutely essential to the Christian life. It's not an add-on or appendage. In fact, first-century Christians would not have conceived of a healthy Christian walk that was unattached from the body life of the local church.

The priority God places on the local church is seen throughout the New Testament. Christ loved the church so much that He "gave himself for it" (Ephesians 5:25) and "purchased [it] with his own blood" (Acts 20:28).

In Acts 2, as three thousand people were added to the church, we see these new believers treating the church at Jerusalem as their hub for spiritual growth and fellowship: "And they continued stedfastly in the apostles' doctrine and fellowship, and in breaking of bread, and in prayers.... And they, continuing daily with one accord in the temple, and breaking bread from house to house, did eat their meat with gladness and singleness of heart" (Acts 2:42, 46).

Of the twenty-one epistles in the New Testament, nine are written to specific local churches, and three are addressed to local church leaders.[1] Thus, over half of the New Testament epistles specifically deal with the organization, operation, and relationships within the local church.

The local church is not only essential to Christ as His plan to reach the world with the gospel (although it is that), but it is essential for *you*. It's the place God has provided for your spiritual growth, maturing, and service.

The more pressure we are under from the outside world, the more we need the strength and encouragement that comes from the fellowship of the local church. Hebrews 10:23–25 connects holding to the truth to assembling with other Christians, and it admonishes us to do both: "Let us hold fast the profession of our faith without wavering; (for he is faithful that promised;) And let us consider one another to provoke unto love and to good works: Not forsaking the assembling of ourselves together, as the manner of some is; but exhorting one another: and so much the more, as ye see the day approaching."

If I were not the pastor of Lancaster Baptist Church, I would still be there every time the doors were open. I need the fellowship, encouragement, prayers, singing, teaching, and preaching for my own life and spiritual health, not just for the sake of the church.

Families need the local church, too. There is no other environment in our culture today that provides ongoing support to strengthen families by reaffirming their necessity and providing biblical teaching for husbands and wives and dads and moms and kids. Children and teens need the church—and this is true no matter what their family makeup is, whether they are in a two-parent or single-parent home. Young people grow in their faith by hearing preaching and seeing multiple generations worship the Lord and live out their faith. Additionally, the church is uniquely positioned to provide mentoring and modeling for young people confused over our culture's undermining of families and blurring gender distinctions.

We have a first-century example of the incredible impact a church can make in an otherwise spiritually-disadvantaged family through Timothy's life. It seems from Acts 16:1–3 that

Timothy's Greek father was not a believer, and possibly out of the picture as well. (Other than this one reference to him in Acts 16, he is not mentioned again.) However, Timothy's mother and grandmother were both godly Christians (2 Timothy 1:5), and Timothy himself heard the Scriptures from an early age (2 Timothy 3:15).

But although Timothy grew up in a pagan culture with either an unbelieving or absent father, he was not destined to become a statistical casualty. The spiritual nurturing he received from his mother and grandmother and apparently the family's involvement in the church Paul planted provided such an environment of growth that Timothy himself went into the ministry. Eventually, Paul would write two epistles—1 and 2 Timothy—to Timothy with pastoral instructions to him about leading a local church.

There will be difficult days ahead for Christians and families as our culture continues throwing off moral restraints and opposing all who object. Discouragement will abound, and weak Christians—disconnected from the body of Christ—won't survive. They will cave and blend in with the culture or become despondent and defeated. Like the first-century churches, we will need to assemble and support one another—to encourage each other and to strengthen one another.

The Local Church Is Personal

Some Christians embrace the concept of "the Church," comprised of all believers, but struggle to commit themselves to the local church of which they are a member.

It is true that there is a wonderful day coming when the Church—with believers from every age and nation—will gather together as the spotless Bride of Christ (Ephesians 5:27). But until then, God's plan is the local church—the physical assembly of saved, baptized believers. And perhaps now, more than ever, it is vital that American Christians commit themselves to this plan.

How do you know if you're committed to the local church?

Are you present when the church gathers?

> *And let us consider one another to provoke unto love and to good works: Not forsaking the assembling of ourselves together, as the manner of some is; but exhorting one another: and so much the more, as ye see the day approaching. (Hebrews 10:24–25)*

Do you use the opportunities God has given you to serve your church family?

> *For, brethren, ye have been called unto liberty; only use not liberty for an occasion to the flesh, but by love*

serve one another.... As we have therefore opportunity, let us do good unto all men, especially unto them who are of the household of faith. (Galatians 5:13, 6:10)

Do you give to support the work of God through the local church?

Now concerning the collection for the saints, as I have given order to the churches of Galatia, even so do ye. Upon the first day of the week let every one of you lay by him in store, as God hath prospered him, that there be no gatherings when I come. (1 Corinthians 16:1–2)

Do you share the gospel alongside your church family?

Go ye therefore, and teach all nations, baptizing them in the name of the Father, and of the Son, and of the Holy Ghost: Teaching them to observe all things whatsoever I have commanded you: and, lo, I am with you alway, even unto the end of the world. Amen. (Matthew 28:19–20)

Are you actively learning and teaching others in the faith?

And the things that thou hast heard of me among many witnesses, the same commit thou to faithful men, who shall be able to teach others also. (2 Timothy 2:2)

Finally, what does it take to pull you away from regularly participating in these basic ways? Your honest answer to that question is a true gauge of your level of commitment to the local church.

5} COUNT THE COST

Jesus never promised the Christian life would be easy, but He did tell us to count the cost of following Him.

Several years ago, Terrie and I were in Scotland and made a stop at Saint Andrews University. We were intrigued by stones on the pavement that formed the initials PH. We looked up and noticed a placard with the following words:

> The initials on the pavement nearby mark the spot where Patrick Hamilton, member of the university, was burned at the stake on 29 February 1528, at the age of 24.

Twenty-four! That's the age I was when I began the pastorate.

I had never heard of Patrick Hamilton before, but as I studied his short life, I learned there was much to admire. He was born into Scottish nobility. At the age of fifteen, he became a Catholic abbot. A year later, he went to the University of Paris to pursue a Master of Arts. While in Paris, Hamilton heard the gospel and trusted Christ as his Savior. When he returned to Scotland with his degree, he began teaching at the University of St. Andrews.

As Hamilton began to share his newfound faith in Christ, he quickly experienced opposition. Catholicism was the state religion, and dissent, let alone gospel evangelism, was not looked upon favorably. Soon he was summoned to a trial for heresy.

Hamilton knew that trial would end in his execution, so he fled to Germany. While there, he further studied his biblical convictions and wrote a doctrinal treatise titled *Patrick's Places*. He could have stayed in Germany, and many urged him to do so. The Reformation had already taken hold there, and there was considerable religious freedom to preach salvation by grace.

But Hamilton couldn't get away from the fact that his family and countrymen did not have the knowledge of the gospel. He counted the cost and returned to Scotland with one purpose in mind: tell everyone he could about Christ in whatever time he had before he would be martyred.

Starting at his brother's house on the western side of the island, Hamilton shared the gospel with his family and saw many relatives come to faith in Christ. From there, he began a short but effective itinerant ministry.

Eventually, Hamilton was invited to return to Saint Andrew's University as a professor and promised the opportunity to preach openly. Hamilton knew the invitation was a ploy to lure him to publicly preach the "heresy" for which he would be arrested. But once again, he counted the cost and decided that the opportunity to preach Christ to his students and the townspeople was worth death.

For five weeks, Hamilton preached the gospel. As he had anticipated, he was arrested, made to stand trial for "heresy," convicted, and burned at the stake—less than four months after having arrived back in Scotland.

Was Hamilton's sacrifice worth it? Was he foolish to not keep his faith secret? Did he miscalculate?

Those questions might be hard to answer if you only value this present world. After all, a man with the gifts and advantages which Hamilton had would surely have gone far in this world.

But Hamilton wasn't living for this world. When he trusted Christ as his Savior, he received a gift too precious to hide—the gift of eternal life. And he received a calling too great to ignore—the calling upon every Christian to share the gospel. And as it turned out, this gift and calling conflicted with the social expectations placed on Hamilton by the religious and governmental leaders of his day. He was aware of what it would cost him, but he decided this life is worth fully investing in the next.

We don't always know the result of such choices. Only eternity will fully reveal the compounded interest of these sacrifices.

In Hamilton's case, there was some immediate fruit. His burning had been particularly gruesome due to green wood and wind blowing the fire away from his body. As a result, he burned for six awful hours. People who had previously heard him preach the gospel saw in those hours the reality of his faith and the grace of God. The result was that so many people responded by trusting Christ that one of Hamilton's adversaries advised against creating any more martyrs at the stake saying, "The reek of master Patrick Hamilton affected all those upon whom it blew."[1]

That comment reminds me of Paul's words in 2 Corinthians 2:15–16 as he explained preaching the gospel to a lost world and said, "For we are unto God a sweet savour of Christ, in them that are saved, and in them that perish: To the one we are the savour of death unto death; and to the other the savour of life unto life." Like Paul,

Patrick Hamilton's message was sweet to those who trusted Christ, and the "sweet savour of Christ" was spread even through his death. But his life, including the way in which he was killed, was a disgusting reek to those who rejected Christ. I'm afraid that many Christians in America today do not have this "reek" because they are ashamed to boldly identify with Christ. They are afraid of what it will cost.

To that end, I'd like to propose three questions to help us count the cost:

Is Religious Persecution Possible in America?

The reality is easily missed today because so many nations now value at least some level of religious freedom, but the United States of America was the forerunner of these principles. And that was largely due to the influence of Baptists. It was Baptists, with their convictions of "individual soul liberty," who emphasized the need for religious freedom in the founding of America.

In the town of Illston, Wales, there is a remaining foundation from the earliest Baptist church in that country. Established there in 1649, it soon relocated to nearby Swansea, Wales. John Myles served as the first pastor until he, along with several members from the church, fled persecution by immigrating to the American colonies. They ended up in Massachusetts, the same state from which the Baptist preacher Roger Williams had been banished for his beliefs. Some twenty years later, however, this group was able to establish a Baptist church—the earliest such church in Massachusetts. In fact, the town of Swansea, Massachusetts, was named after this church and its hometown in Wales. It was also one of the first towns in Massachusetts founded on the premise of religious liberty for all.

You may remember, too, from American history that it was the Baptists and their concern for religious liberty that led to the First Amendment to our Constitution and guaranteed every American religious liberty.[2]

But religious liberty on a document and religious liberty in practice are not the same. And while Americans have enjoyed a level of religious liberty of which Christians in previous millennia could not have dreamed, the underpinnings of that liberty are quickly eroding today.

Consider the following instances:

- Jack Phillips, owner of Masterpiece Cakeshop in Colorado, won a Supreme Court case for his right to deny baking a wedding cake for a gay couple. Currently, he is being sued by a transgender woman for refusing to bake a pink and blue cake honoring her transition. Phillips lost in the appeals court and has taken the case to the Colorado Supreme Court, which is now deliberating.[3] Phillips is willing to bake standard cakes for anyone, including those suing him. His refusal is only for cakes celebrating events that go against his conscience; and for that, activists have targeted him for multiple lawsuits.

- Joe Kennedy, a high school football coach in Washington state, made a practice of briefly kneeling on the field in prayer after football games. Many of his players asked to join him. When the practice was brought (by an opposing team) to the attention of his school board, he was fired. After a lengthy, seven-year legal battle, which Coach Kennedy fought for the sake of religious liberty, the Supreme Court ruled in his favor.[4]
- Five men and one woman who participated in a protest outside an abortion clinic in Mt. Juliet, Tennessee, were convicted of "felony conspiracy and violating the FACE Act," apparently for peacefully singing hymns at an abortion clinic. What makes this situation more concerning is that no arrests were made the day of the protest. It wasn't until October 2022—seventeen months later—that the federal government swooped in with arrests.[5]

These threats to religious liberty are not just here in the United States. In other countries which we would normally assume to have modern religious liberty, this is happening as well.

- In December 2022, Isabel Vaughan-Spruce, director of the UK March for Life, stood across the street from the Birmingham abortion center and silently prayed. Police forces approached her and questioned if she was praying. When she responded, "I might be praying in my head," she was arrested.[6]
- In Canada, Pastor Tim Stephens of Fairview Baptist Church, Alberta, was arrested twice in 2021 for holding church services. In the second instance, a police helicopter was dispatched on a Sunday morning to find the church's outdoor services, and the next day the police arrested him. He was held in jail for over two weeks because he refused to accept the conditions of his bail—that he promise to not hold church services. Eventually, he was acquitted—for obvious reasons.

There are Christians who deny that situations like these are instances of religious persecution. They essentially point to the technical aspects of law or policy that these individuals violated and suggest the Christians in question were just being obstinate.

But this approach misses the obvious motive behind these cases. The technical aspects cited are *aimed* at silencing dissent. Their very purpose is intended to silence or mitigate the influence of Christians. The fact that they happen at all shows a devaluing of sincerely-held religious beliefs in places that used to value religious freedom.

There are times when Christians have to choose between obeying God or government. And those choices are not always as obvious as a direct "yes or no, do you deny Jesus?" question. Sometimes they are more veiled attempts by those who have or want to have power to prohibit the spread of the gospel or silence the expression of faith. When there is a conflict between human authority and God's instructions, we must, with Peter and the other apostles, determine, "We ought to obey God rather than men" (Acts 5:29).

A kind of grasping for control is happening today in America, and it is on the basis of forcing an aggressive LGBTQ agenda. For years now, LGBTQ activists have worked to link sexual orientation and gender identity into existing laws that prohibit discrimination based on race or gender. From here, it is a simple step to rule that anyone who simply states the Bible truths about sex, marriage, and gender will be engaging in hate speech. Already, laws are being passed in multiple states to the effect that parents do not need to be told when their young children are transitioning to a different gender and that parents who stand in the way of such transitions will lose custody of their children. These are extreme measures, and they show how intolerant the LGBTQ lobby is of opposing views.

I share all this to say that Bible-believing Christians need to be aware of the significance of this agenda and be prepared to unequivocally state the truths of God's Word, regardless of the results. Particularly, we need to be willing to say what the Bible says about sin that we might declare what the Bible says about salvation.

Some well-meaning Christians want to dismiss standing on these issues, suggesting that they are peripheral to the gospel. But even in the book of Romans—the great theological treatise on salvation—the apostle Paul addresses the godlessness of culture (specifically, as we saw in chapter 1, related to sexual deviations) as a rebellion against God and thus relevant to the need for the gospel (Romans 1:26–28).

As these matters increasingly become the eye of the needle through which anti-God agendas are pushed and Christians are marginalized or persecuted, we must be convinced that taking a stand in these very areas *is* taking a stand for Christ.

What Can We Do?

So what should we do today, right now, in relation to the unfolding persecution?

Pray for those who are currently persecuted. According to the international Christian persecution watchdog group Open Doors, an average of at least 13 Christians were killed for their faith per day in 2023 for a total of 4,998. The same report warns that more than 365 million (one in seven) Christians face high levels of persecution for their faith.[7]

As Christians around the world suffer for their faith in Christ, we should "Remember them that are in bonds, as bound with them; and them which suffer adversity, as being yourselves also in the body" (Hebrews 13:3). Additionally, American Christians should look to their example and be encouraged in the grace God provides to stand strong for Christ in the face of persecution.

Keep a Gospel-minded perspective. The worldview of the average person has profoundly shifted over the past ten years. A recent poll concluded that twenty-six percent of adults in the US and fifty-two percent of adults in Great Britain do not even believe in God.[8]

Our world needs the gospel like never before. Your city needs the gospel. Now is not the time for Christians to shift our focus to politically-correct social issues or terminology that we perceive will make us more received by our culture. The apostle Paul, who boldly counted the cost in the middle of two political forces that hated him—the Roman government and the Jewish Sanhedrin—kept a gospel perspective: "For the preaching of the cross is to them that perish foolishness; but unto us which are saved it is the power of God" (1 Corinthians 1:18). "For I am not ashamed of the gospel of Christ: for it is the power of God unto salvation to every one that believeth; to the Jew first, and also to the Greek" (Romans 1:16).

Count the cost. Jesus never promised the Christian life would be easy. In fact, He specifically told us it would be hard (John 16:33), and He specifically told us to count the cost of following Him.

> *For which of you, intending to build a tower, sitteth not down first, and counteth the cost, whether he have sufficient to finish it? Lest haply, after he hath laid the foundation, and is not able to finish it, all that behold it begin to mock him, Saying, This man began to build, and was not able to finish.... So likewise, whosoever he*

be of you that forsaketh not all that he hath, he cannot be my disciple. (Luke 14:28–30, 33)

I don't know what persecution may come to Christians in the United States. I pray for a national spiritual awakening that could, at least temporarily, stem the tide of wickedness in our land. But as Christians around the world suffer and are even martyred for their faith, we shouldn't be unwilling to do the same.

I doubt that the cost we are called to make will begin with a gun to the head and a command to deny Christ. It will be—indeed, as mentioned above, it has been—more subtle than that. The temptation to compromise the truth doesn't necessarily come in a single moment of obvious martyrdom. It often comes in a series of decisions that an uncommitted Christian can explain away:

- "I believe the Bible says homosexuality is a sin; I just choose not to preach about it lest I offend those who need Christ."
- "I *personally* believe what the Bible says about XYZ issue, but I can't point to Scripture as my source of conviction in discussion with my unsaved family, lest they ridicule me and don't want to hear the gospel."

- "I know the LGBTQ movement is ungodly, but I feel I should put up the 'pride' flag in my cubical so I don't come under pressure from my boss."

Sometimes our hesitation to count the cost and pay the price is that we value ourselves so greatly and value Jesus so little. The apostle Paul can be an example to us here. As he faced certain persecution, he told the pastors of Ephesus that he knew in every city he would go, "bonds and afflictions abide me." But in the same breath, he continued, "But none of these things move me, neither count I my life dear unto myself, so that I might finish my course with joy, and the ministry, which I have received of the Lord Jesus, to testify the gospel of the grace of God" (Acts 20:23–24).

How Much Is It Worth?

If, when considering the current cultural landscape and the road ahead for our country, our question is, "How much will it *cost* to stand for Christ?" we are asking the wrong question. The question that we should be asking is, "How much is it *worth?*"

Your stand and my stand for Christ—regardless of what it costs—is worth everything. This is because *Jesus* is worth everything.

The realization that Jesus is worth everything was the eventual conclusion of Thomas Cranmer, the Archbishop of Canterbury from 1533–1555. During this politically and religiously tumultuous period of English history, the State Church of England (and the office of the Archbishop of Canterbury with it) went from Catholic to Protestant and back to Catholic in fewer than twenty years and under the reign of three monarchs. Cranmer, who apparently became a born-again Christian early in his tenure, tried to ride this political upheaval without losing his job or, more importantly, his head. During those years, he was hesitant to take bold stands for his faith.

But when Queen Mary I, known as "Bloody Mary" for her persecution of Protestants, ascended to the throne in 1553, she targeted Cranmer. He was arrested and then held in solitary confinement for seventeen months before his trial. When Hugh Latimer and Nicolas Ridley, Cranmer's friends, were burned at the stake for similar charges as Cranmer, Cranmer was forced to witness their burning.

Perhaps it was the long months of solitary confinement. Perhaps it was his lack of strong stands in the past. Perhaps it was sheer terror at what he had witnessed in Latimer and Ridley's executions, but when Cranmer was finally convicted of heresy and then given the opportunity to recant his beliefs, he did. He signed every paper put in front of him and professed his sincere regret for departing from the Catholic Church and authority of the pope.

A final ultimatum was put before Cranmer to publicly recant at the University Church in Oxford, reading a pre-approved statement. But as Cranmer faced the group assembled to listen, he changed his statement. Instead of confessing the "errors" of his gospel-ways, he confessed his regret that he had ever signed a recantation at all. His last words before being pulled from the pulpit were, "And as for the Pope, I refuse him, as Christ's enemy, and Antichrist with all his false doctrine."[9]

Cranmer was then led to the very spot where Latimer and Ridley had been burnt and was similarly martyred. In a final witness to the supremacy and sufficiency of Christ, Cranmer thrust his right hand which had previously signed the statement of recantation into the flames saying, "This hand hath offended." His dying words were, "Lord Jesus, receive my spirit. I see the heavens open and Jesus standing at the right hand of God."

Do you think Cranmer, who is this very moment in the physical presence of Christ, is glad he finally counted the cost and took his stand? Do you think he has any regret over the price he paid for his Savior? I think if he could speak to us today, he would tell us to count the cost and be willing to suffer sooner rather than later. Because whatever the cost, Jesus is worth it.

None of us know what the cost will be. But we know it is worth it.

6} LIVE WITH A CONSISTENT TESTIMONY

To make a difference in this world, live every day for the glory of God.

Harry Ironside's father died in 1878 when Harry was just two years old. After graduating from eighth grade, Harry went to work to help support the family. He got a job with a shoe cobbler who was a devout Christian man. Ironside's task was to pound the leather for the bottom of the shoes after it was soaked and cut to shape. It was a long and tedious task.

There was another cobbler in town who skipped that step, using wet leather for the soles. Ironside asked him about it, and he pointed out that though the quality was less, it created return business because his customers had to come back for repairs.

When Ironside suggested this measure to his boss, he rejected it—not for financial reasons but for spiritual ones. Ironside wrote, "Mr. Mackay stopped his work and opened his Bible. 'Harry,' he said, 'I do not cobble shoes just for the four bits and six bits that I get from my customers. I expect to see every shoe I have ever repaired in a big pile at the judgment seat of Christ, and I do not want the Lord to say to me in that day, 'Dan, this was a poor job. You did not do your best here.' I want Him to be able to say, 'Well done, good and faithful servant.'"

Ironside, who went on to pastor the Moody Church in Chicago and write Bible commentaries I use today, reflected on this experience: "It was a lesson I have never been able to forget. Often when I have been tempted to carelessness and to slipshod effort, I have thought of dear, devoted Dan Mackay, and it has stirred me up to seek to do all as for Him who died to redeem me."[1]

Perhaps it was this experience that Ironside thought of when he said, "If lips and life do not agree, the testimony will not amount to much."[2]

If we are to make a difference for Christ, if our stand for truth will count and our sharing of the gospel will pierce hearts, our lives must match our message. Without a consistent Christian testimony, our own lives will discredit the truths we attempt to share. But when our message is coupled with godly living, it stands as a breathing testimony to the reality of God's grace.

Think of Stephen who, even as he was unjustly accused and made to stand for a sham trial before being stoned to death for his faith, offered forgiveness to his accusers. The sincerity of his heart and genuineness of his love was so great that *those who hated him* "were not able to resist the wisdom and the spirit by which he spake" (Acts 6:10).

This kind of testimony isn't chosen in the moment of need. It is lived out day by day as we walk with the Lord. A consistent testimony isn't so much built by what we *do* as it is by who we *are.* There are three simple *being* instructions to remember: Be sincere. Be aware. Be ready.

Be Sincere

The word *sincere* comes from the Latin words *sine,* meaning "without" and *cera,* meaning "wax." Put together, it means "without wax." The story goes that merchants selling pottery would sometimes fill in cracks with wax and then paint the entire vessel, concealing the repairs. No one knew the difference until they were using the vessel and the wax melted—either in the sun or in the oven. Reputable merchants, however, would hang a sign at their shops reading "Sincere"—*without wax.*

As growing Christians, we recognize that being transformed into the image of Christ is the process of a lifetime. We will never be perfect this side of Heaven, and that is not our goal. But we should be *sincere.* There is a difference between imperfection, which is the reality of all humans, and hypocrisy, which is pretending to be something we are not.

A hypocritical Christian professes to believe one way, but his own life reveals the opposite. This is the Christian who publicly decries the immorality of our culture but secretly indulges his lust with pornography. This is the Christian who professes to believe in the sanctity of marriage but then leaves his wife. The world loves to mock the moral failures of Christians. They point to the hypocrisy of believers as a form of proof that we don't value the beliefs that we say we do . . . and they have a point.

Paul wrote to the Philippian church, "Do all things without murmurings and disputings: That ye may be blameless and harmless, the sons of God, without rebuke, in the midst of a crooked and perverse nation, among whom ye shine as lights in the world" (Philippians 2:14–15). Our ability to shine as lights for the Lord is directly connected to our testimonies. My friend and mentor, Pastor Bobby Roberson, used to say about our gospel witness and testimony, "I don't have to worry about keeping the light shining; I just have to keep the bulb clean."

Integrity matters in life, and it especially matters for Christians. The apostle Paul was able to say to Timothy, who had extensively traveled with him and observed his life close-up, "But thou hast fully known my doctrine, *manner of life,* purpose, faith, longsuffering, charity, patience..." (2 Timothy 3:10). The words that Timothy heard Paul speak when he was sharing the gospel did not conflict with the words that Timothy heard Paul speak when he was in a wayside inn. Paul was certainly not perfect, but he was consistent.

As we saw in our previous chapter, godly Christians should expect to suffer for their faith. This is seen all throughout the New Testament, especially in the book of 1 Peter. Interestingly, however, as Peter shares the reality of suffering for the faith, he gives a warning: make sure you are suffering for Christ, not for sinfulness on your part.

> *Beloved, think it not strange concerning the fiery trial which is to try you, as though some strange thing happened unto you: But rejoice, inasmuch as ye are partakers of Christ's sufferings; that, when his glory shall be revealed, ye may be glad also with exceeding joy. If ye be reproached for the name of Christ, happy*

> *are ye; for the spirit of glory and of God resteth upon you: on their part he is evil spoken of, but on your part he is glorified. But let none of you suffer as a murderer, or as a thief, or as an evildoer, or as a busybody in other men's matters. Yet if any man suffer as a Christian, let him not be ashamed; but let him glorify God on this behalf. (1 Peter 4:12–16)*

In other words, suffering for Christ is noble, but suffering for sin is avoidable. So make sure that your walk matches your talk.

Be Aware

During the Sydney Olympic Games in 2000, the great Kenyan runner Bernard "Kip" Lagat was interviewed. At one point the reporter asked him how it was that his country produced so many champion distance runners. With a smile and clever wit, Lagat replied that they had a special motivation in his nation for success in running. He said, "It's the road signs: 'Beware of Lions.'"

The reality is that there is an enemy stalking every believer every day. It is Satan, and the Bible warns us that he is constantly on the prowl and out to destroy. "Be sober, be vigilant; because your adversary the devil, as a roaring lion, walketh about, seeking whom he may devour"

(1 Peter 5:8). Like a lion, the devil desires to destroy us and render us ineffective for God's service.

There is no permanent victory in spiritual warfare. There is no day of the week that we can let our guard down. Satan works "to steal, and to kill, and to destroy" (John 10:10). Satan actively and persistently targets the child of God with temptation—so much so, that one of his names is even "the tempter" (Matthew 4:3).

We should not let these warnings discourage us, for God has given us every resource we need to fight temptation. Second Corinthians 10:4 tells us that the weapons at our disposal are "mighty through God to the pulling down of strong holds." But we should take the warnings seriously.

Are there areas in life where you know you are susceptible to temptation? Do what you can to avoid temptation in those areas as Romans 13:14 says: "But put ye on the Lord Jesus Christ, and make not provision for the flesh, to fulfil the lusts thereof." And for the instances of temptation you cannot avoid, equip yourself ahead with spiritual ammunition—specific verses from the Word of God. Psalm 119:11 instructs and encourages, "Thy word have I hid in mine heart, that I might not sin against thee.

Are there areas in your life where you are struggling with habitual sin? Enlist the help of a godly Christian to pray with you about it, find the root cause, and provide accountability to combat it. James 5:16 instructs, "Confess your faults one to another, and pray one for another, that ye may be healed. The effectual fervent prayer of a righteous man availeth much."

The amazing grace of God that saves us and cleanses us from all of our sin also gives us the power to walk in daily holiness. Titus 2:11–12 says, "For the grace of God that bringeth salvation hath appeared to all men, Teaching us that, denying ungodliness and worldly lusts, we should live soberly, righteously, and godly, in this present world." God's grace gives us the power to deny ungodliness—to say no to sin.

I love the phrase in the passage above that says we can walk godly *in this present world.* Even in this book, we've seen glimpses of the evil of this world. Sometimes Christians believe the lie that the ungodliness surrounding them is so great that they cannot live in spiritual victory. That is simply not true. God's powerful grace is available to enable you and me to say "no" to sin and "yes" to the Holy Spirit moment by moment. First Corinthians 10:13 assures us, "There hath no temptation taken you but such as is common to man: but God is faithful, who will not suffer you to be tempted above that ye are able; but will with the temptation also make a way to escape, that ye may be able to bear it."

Be Ready

President John F. Kennedy frequently used historical anecdotes to illustrate his speeches. One of his favorites dated back to the American Revolution. In 1780, with the fate of the country still hanging in the balance as the war with England continued, the Connecticut House of Representatives meeting was in session. Suddenly the sky darkened ominously, even though it was the middle of the day. Some feared it was a sign of coming judgment and called for the body to be adjourned. But the Speaker of the House, Colonel Davenport, rose and said, "The Day of Judgment is either approaching, or it is not. If it is not, there is no cause for adjournment. If it is, I choose to be found doing my duty. Therefore, I wish that candles be brought."

Jesus promised us that He would return: "In my Father's house are many mansions:...I go to prepare a place for you. And if I go and prepare a place for you, I will come again, and receive you unto myself; that where I am, there ye may be also" (John 14:2–3).

The reality that Jesus is coming back is one of the most powerful motivations that we have to live with a godly testimony. The apostle John wrote, "Beloved, now are we the sons of God, and it doth not yet appear what we shall be: but we know that, when he shall appear, we shall be like him; for we shall see him as he is. *And every man that hath this hope in him purifieth himself,* even as he is pure" (1 John 3:2–3).

Every day, we should live with anticipation for Christ's return. This includes living in such a way "when he shall appear, we may have confidence, and not be ashamed before him at his coming" (1 John 2:28).

Live for the Glory of God

All three of these—to be sincere, be aware, and be ready—are summed up in the goal of every Christian: to live every day for the glory of God.

Some Christians think that glorifying God is something we do on Sundays. Or that glorifying God through the week is a job for pastors and others in vocational ministry.

But Paul made it clear that living for the glory of God is the everyday opportunity of every child of God, even in the most mundane areas of life: "Whether therefore ye eat, or drink, or whatsoever ye do, do all to the glory of God" (1 Corinthians 10:31).

That was really the message Dan Mackay tried to convey to the young Harry Ironside as he refused to cut corners in his business. And it is the message you can live every day.

People may falsely accuse us. We may be called to suffer for Christ. But regardless of the vitriol hurled against us or evil surrounding us, may we live a consistent Christian testimony for the glory of the God who is within us. He is worthy.

7} TEACH THE NEXT GENERATION

We must invest in transferring truth to the hearts of young people.

Most Americans who know the name Ronald Reagan, remember him as the fortieth President of the United States. As a Californian, however, I also remember him as the Governor of California during my childhood. It was, in fact, during his 1967 Inaugural Address for his first term as governor that he made this memorable statement about freedom: "Freedom is a fragile thing and it's never more than one generation away from extinction. It is not ours by way of inheritance; it must be fought for and defended constantly by each generation."

The fragility of freedom and the need to pass it to the next generation is one of the reasons to teach children patriotism. It's why we must give our own children and the young people in our churches and Christian schools an accurate understanding of the Christian values that shaped our nation, a love for all that is good and right about our country, and a conviction that freedom is worth defending.

But as important as it is to teach these values to American young people, they need more. They need to know the truths of God's Word. They need a Christian identity in an anti-Christian world.

I want to be clear here: I don't believe the gospel is one generation from extinction. I don't believe that the perpetuation of the church hinges on our faithfulness as parents. God has explicitly promised that He personally will preserve His Word to all generations (Psalm 12:6–7, Psalm 119:89). Jesus promised, "I will build my church; and the gates of hell shall not prevail against it" (Matthew 16:18). Historically, we see that God has continued His work on Earth and preserved His truth even when individual churches, families, or nations have failed.

But if I care about the perpetuation of truth in my family, church, and culture (and I care about it deeply), I must invest in the next generation. I must give them the gospel. I must teach them to love God and to identify with Him and His truth. I cannot neglect the transfer of truth to those who are coming after me.

This transfer was a passion of the apostle Paul who wrote to his "son in the faith" Timothy, "And the things that thou hast heard of me among many witnesses, the same commit thou to faithful men, who shall be able to teach others also" (2 Timothy 2:2).

The Assault on Today's Youth

The world and the devil are actively fighting for the hearts of the next generation of Christians. For decades, there has been a carefully-crafted agenda underway to indoctrinate and recruit young people to ungodly lifestyles and to convince them that God's ways are harsh, judgmental, and inapplicable to the age in which we live.

I recently stood at Nuremberg, Germany, where Adolf Hitler held huge rallies for the Nazi Party. At one of these rallies, some two thousand German youth marched from all parts of Germany to participate.

In his "Speech to the German Youth" address at a youth rally in Berlin, Hitler spoke these words: "When an opponent declares, 'I will not come over to your side,' I calmly say, 'Your child belongs to us already.... What are you? You will pass on. Your descendants, however, now stand in the new camp. In a short time they will know nothing else but this new community.'"[1] This is a similar mentality with which LGBTQ activists work to gain acceptance and approval for their cause in the hearts and minds of young people. If they—through entertainment, education systems, popular culture, and outright assaults on parental rights—can break down the transfer of values and truth from parents to children, they can capture a generation for their cause. And they are busy about doing it.

Allow me to provide a few examples—from California to Florida to Missouri, and right down to the bookshelves of your public library:

- In Los Angeles County, the LA Unified School District lists a campaign for LGBTQ-related events nearly every month of the school year, including bookending the year with August as "Queer All Year kickoff" and June as "National Pride Month." Other "special days" include "National Coming Out Day" in October and "Solidarity Week" in November.[2]
- Disneyland recently hosted its second annual "Pride Nite," a festival to honor the LGBTQ+ community. Tickets were available to children as young as *three years old*. The park was filled with LGBTQ-themed celebration opportunities, including rainbow food items, photo spots, and characters promoting the LGBTQ agenda.[3]

- Olivia Rodrigo, a popular singer and songwriter whose target audience is teenagers and young women, provides free condoms and Plan B pills with pro-choice messaging at concerts. (And for those who think living in a more conservative state avoids these problems, she did this at a concert in St. Louis, Missouri—a state with one of the strictest anti-abortion laws in place.)[4]
- Children's author Philip Pullman whose teen fiction fantasy trilogy *His Dark Materials* has sold over 17.5 million copies, boldly proclaimed, "If there is a God, and he is as the Christians describe him, then he deserves to be put down and rebelled against."[5] In one interview about the impact of his books on young people, he said, "My books are about killing God."[6]
- The California Legislature passed and Gavin Newsom signed into law AB1955, which prohibits school districts from notifying parents if their child has asked everyone at school to use a different name and pronouns. This law is designed to create division between parents and children, propagating confusion regarding God's creation of male and female.

Frankly, these five examples are simply provided because they are recent. In any single week, you can find similar news stories of assaults on the beliefs and morality of young people.

What are Christians to do in the face of this evil? They are to do what God commanded thousands of years ago—they are to purposefully transfer the truth to young people.

The Responsibility to Transfer Truth

Although God created human government, He did not give government the responsibility to raise children. This responsibility is given directly to parents.

It is critical that Christian parents instill the Word of God into the hearts of their children. This is God's plan for protecting a child and shaping the future of a nation.

> *And these words, which I command thee this day, shall be in thine heart: And thou shalt teach them diligently unto thy children, and shalt talk of them when thou sittest in thine house, and when thou walkest by the way, and when thou liest down, and when thou risest up. And thou shalt bind them for a sign upon thine hand, and they shall be as frontlets between thine eyes. And thou shalt write them upon the posts of thy house, and on thy gates. (Deuteronomy 6:6–9)*

Parents are to teach God's Word *diligently* and *frequently.* This requires that it is real in the hearts of the parents, and it requires intention and sacrifice.

Wise parents need to be on guard, aware of and setting boundaries for what they will allow their children to see, hear, sing, and share with others. They need to know what their children are being taught in school, what is influencing them, and who their friends are. There needs to be careful filtering in place so that things do not slip through the cracks of the defenses you have set up around your home.

What's more, Christian parents need to model the biblical design for the family to their children. Young people need to see their dads treat their moms with deference, love, care, and respect. They need to see a healthy marriage relationship and observe that love is not all about having a partner who brings sensual satisfaction but about fulfillment in a commitment to a spouse and obedience to God. If you are a single parent, remember that one of the blessings of being part of a church family is that your children will have opportunity to see these examples in other Christian families in the church.

This brings us to the other institution God has ordained and instructed to invest in young people—the local church. The church is to share the gospel with every person (Mark 16:15) and disciple all Christians (Matthew 28:20). In both instances, this includes young people.

Bible-believing churches are a powerful help to Christian parents in coming alongside and supporting families, and they are also a primary means to transfer truth. As children and teens hear Bible preaching and see godly role models in a church family, they are influenced in ways that build up, supplement, and extend beyond what a home can provide. And for children who do not have Christian parents, churches can also reach out with the gospel and discipleship.

Just as parents must accept their God-given responsibility to teach the truths of God's Word to their children, so churches must accept their responsibility to give substantive truth to the next generation. Fun events and activities have their place (an important place), but there must be an overarching purpose in children and teen ministries to evangelize and disciple. Children should be learning about God and His Word at church. And teens should be becoming grounded in Bible doctrine and learning the truths of God's Word that counter the lies of our current culture.

Another way that churches provide discipleship of young people is through Christian education. Effective Christian schools not only serve to protect young people from the ungodly agendas that are increasingly being pushed through public schools, but they provide an environment to nurture hearts for God as they teach academic subjects from a God-honoring, Christian worldview.

The Fortification of Truth

As discouraging as the assault on young people is, we can take courage from the biblical examples of young people who stood for God and truth in godless environments. Let's look at Timothy, Moses, Daniel, and an unnamed Israelite maid who all show the difference that even a little godly influence can have in a child's life.

Earlier in this book, we considered Timothy, whose Greek father was apparently an unbeliever. Yet even growing up in the ungodly, sensual Greek culture, Timothy's mother and grandmother so instilled God's Word and biblical truth into his heart that he held fast to the faith. In 2 Timothy, the Apostle Paul made two references to the early training in Timothy's life by his mother and grandmother: "When I call to remembrance the unfeigned faith that is in thee, which dwelt first in thy grandmother Lois, and thy mother Eunice; and I am persuaded that in thee also.... And that from a child thou hast known the holy scriptures, which are able to make thee wise unto salvation through faith which is in Christ Jesus" (2 Timothy 1:5, 3:15).

In the Old Testament, we see Moses, who only had a short time—a few years at most—with his mother (Exodus 2:7–10). Yet, when he came of age, the values and his identity as one of God's people which his mother Jocabed had instilled into his young heart guided his choices: "By faith Moses, when he was come to years, refused to be called the son of Pharaoh's daughter; Choosing rather to suffer affliction with the people of God, than to enjoy the pleasures of sin for a season" (Hebrews 11:24–25).

Then there was the Israelite girl who was captured by the Syrians and taken to serve as a slave in the house of the Syrian general Naaman. This young girl who had been ripped from her home and godly influences had such a deep faith and commitment to God instilled in her heart that when she learned that Naaman had leprosy, she told his wife that the prophet Elisha would be able to heal him. Her faith is particularly amazing when you consider that Elisha had never healed a leper before. (See Luke 4:27.) She had been brought up to believe that God's power working through God's man could accomplish the impossible.

And who can forget Daniel? Taken captive as a teenager to Babylon and placed under unimaginable pressure to compromise, he took a strong stand for God. Daniel 1:8 records, "But Daniel purposed in his heart that he would not defile himself with the portion of the king's meat, nor with the wine which he drank: therefore he requested of the prince of the eunuchs that he might not defile himself."

From these examples, we can also summarize a few crucial ways we need to teach the next generation.

Teach the way of salvation. As vital as Lois and Eunice's roll was in teaching Timothy the Scriptures, don't miss the purpose in teaching the Scriptures—salvation. The goal of transferring truth to young people isn't moral kids who don't know God. It is that young people trust Christ as their Savior and experience the powerful grace of God at work in their lives. It is that, through the indwelling Holy Spirit, they live fruitful, Christ-focused lives.

If you are a parent or grandparent, I encourage you to pray every day for your children and grandchildren's salvation. Teach them the gospel. Help them see their need for a Savior. And be ready to lead them to faith in Christ.

If you are a Christian who works with young people in any way—as a Sunday school teacher, school teacher, coach, etc.—I encourage you also to remember that the fundamental need in every person's life is salvation through Christ. If you are teaching or influencing in a Christian environment, mention the gospel often, and make it your goal to know whether or not each young person under your care has trusted Christ as his or her Savior. If you are teaching or influencing in a secular environment, pray diligently for opportunities to share the gospel in one-on-one settings.

Teach the Scriptures. The only way young people will be able to stand against the laws of our culture is if they know the truth of Christ—not what their parents or youth workers know and believe, but what they have internalized for themselves.

Teach God's Word in your home. Start with something as basic as regular family devotions. It doesn't have to be complicated. In fact, keeping it simple will help you stay consistent. Just purpose to take some time every day to teach the Word of God to your children.

In our home as our children were growing up, this was usually me reading a chapter or a few verses from Proverbs during breakfast. I wanted to give our kids truths to carry throughout their day. However you do it, make sure your children hear you talk about God and about the Word of God.

Charles Spurgeon said, "Brethren, I wish it were more common, I wish it were universal, with all [Christians] to have family prayer. We sometimes hear of children of Christian parents who do not grow up in the fear of God, and we are asked how it is that they turn out so badly. In many, very many cases, I fear there is such a neglect of family worship that it's not probable that the children are at all impressed by any piety supposed to be possessed by their parents."

And, as Deuteronomy 6:7 instructs, teach God's Word to your children *throughout* the day: "talk of them when thou sittest in thine house, and when thou walkest by the way, and when thou liest down, and when thou risest up." Look for moments in all kinds of interaction with your children to bring their attention to God and His Word, to relate their questions or experiences to what the Bible says.

Teach them to stand for Christ. What makes the stories of Moses, the captured Israelite girl, and Daniel so remarkable is that they were prepared to take a stand for God when their parents and mentors were not present. Teach these stories to your children. Teach them what to do when they are tempted by evil. Teach them how to respond when they are in situations in which God is mocked. Teach them how to have the courage to stand for Christ even if they must stand alone.

Ecclesiastes 4:12 tells us that "a threefold cord is not quickly broken." Like a strong rope made of multiple cords, good influences weave together in the hearts of children to bring stability and keep them from evil. I believe that a godly family who is faithful in a biblical church and working with a Christian school makes a strong trio for raising Christ-centered children.

Yes, our young people are targeted with an ungodly agenda. Yes, they are vulnerable to harmful influences. But, as parents and grandparents, as pastors and teachers, God has given us powerful influence into their hearts. It's up to us to seize it.

8} ENGAGE AS A CITIZEN

Christians live as dual citizens of their nation and their heavenly Home.

You might think from the emphasis I've placed throughout these pages on non-political issues, that I don't engage in politics. You would be incorrect. I believe strongly that Christians in free nations have a responsibility to do what they can to preserve religious freedom. And I believe that American Christians have the unique opportunity to engage in the processes that can help preserve our freedoms.

The extremes among Christians when it comes to political issues is to either engage so passionately that we set our hope in government or political movements, or to become so passive that we fail our children and grandchildren. Neither extreme is godly.

In this final chapter, I would like to take a look at our responsibility from three vantage points: a biblical view, a practical view, and a heavenly view.

A Biblical View

It isn't coincidental that the rise in globalist thinking and anti-patriotism tends to come from those who reject biblical truth.

Perhaps because Americans have been blessed for so long with a country established on Christian values, American Christians easily assume that it is that foundation alone that calls for patriotism. Thus, as they see our nation's Christian values erode (which is undoubtedly happening), it's easy to assume that love for country may thus be unfounded. But that thought process is not biblical.

Both government and the concept of individual nations were instituted by God. We can see the importance of both in a quick Bible study:

Shortly after Noah and his family stepped off the ark, God instituted civil government (Genesis 9:6). The Bible explicitly states in Romans 13 that government is ordained by God and is necessary for the punishment of evildoers.

> *Let every soul be subject unto the higher powers. For there is no power but of God: the powers that be are*

ordained of God. Whosoever therefore resisteth the power, resisteth the ordinance of God: and they that resist shall receive to themselves damnation. For rulers are not a terror to good works, but to the evil. Wilt thou then not be afraid of the power? do that which is good, and thou shalt have praise of the same: For he is the minister of God to thee for good. But if thou do that which is evil, be afraid; for he beareth not the sword in vain: for he is the minister of God, a revenger to execute wrath upon him that doeth evil. (Romans 13:1–4)

God also ordained nations.

These are the families of the sons of Noah, after their generations, in their nations: and by these were the nations divided in the earth after the flood. (Genesis 10:32)

God, as the Sovereign Ruler of all, displays His power by setting up and bringing down nations.

He increaseth the nations, and destroyeth them: he enlargeth the nations, and straiteneth them again. (Job 12:23)

> *And he changeth the times and the seasons: he removeth kings, and setteth up kings: he giveth wisdom unto the wise, and knowledge to them that know understanding: (Daniel 2:21)*

The time and space boundaries of nations reveal the power of God and point people to seek after God.

> *And hath made of one blood all nations of men for to dwell on all the face of the earth, and hath determined the times before appointed, and the bounds of their habitation; That they should seek the Lord, if haply they might feel after him, and find him, though he be not far from every one of us: (Acts 17:26–27)*

The one-world government during the Tribulation will be led by the Antichrist ("the beast" in Revelation 13) who is given power by Satan in blatant rejection of God's right to rule. This government will include a one-world currency in which to participate people must receive "the mark of the beast."[1]

> *And the beast which I saw was like unto a leopard, and his feet were as the feet of a bear, and his mouth as the mouth of a lion: and the dragon gave him his power, and his seat, and great authority. . . . And he opened his mouth in blasphemy against God, to blaspheme*

> *his name, and his tabernacle, and them that dwell in heaven.... And he causeth all, both small and great, rich and poor, free and bond, to receive a mark in their right hand, or in their foreheads: And that no man might buy or sell, save he that had the mark, or the name of the beast, or the number of his name. (Revelation 13:2, 6, 16–17)*

These points are a high-end overview, but what I want to emphasize is that because God ordained human government within individual nations, patriotism for one's country is appropriate for the Christian. That is true regardless of the country in which one lives.

Of course, patriotism becomes a more complex issue under oppressive governments. Christians in first-century Rome probably experienced patriotism differently than we do today. (To make it even more complex, many of those Christians were not Roman-born, but were conquered peoples.) But this doesn't mean that Christians in oppressive nations do not long for the flourishing of their country. I personally know Christians from countries such as China, Iran, Yemen, and other extremely-oppressive places. These godly people suffer under their government's persecution of Christians, but they still long to see their country flourish in freedom and economic prosperity—not just personally, but patriotically.

So we should be careful about assuming that the decline of morality in America allows for a decline in patriotism. In reality, our love of country should burn brighter the more we see it in danger.

And what about Christian participation in the political arena? There are those who argue that since we don't see Christians in the New Testament shaping laws or policies, it is unbiblical for Christians to do that today. Some even go so far as to say that heart-felt engagement in these ways is idolatrous or that it somehow negates our faithfulness to live as pilgrims on this earth with a view to our heavenly home.

These concerns are easily answered in understanding that the Bible was written for all Christians in every time and place. Naturally, then, it would not include specific instructions for modern Christians in free nations on voting or engaging in ways Christians in other times and places never could. What we do see in the New Testament, however, is that Paul, who never had the opportunity to elect government officials as we do here in the United States, was very willing to use his rights as a Roman citizen. On one occasion he used these rights to have false accusations publicly expunged (Acts 16:37–38). On another occasion, Paul used his citizenship to avoid a beating (Acts 22:25–26).

American Christians live in a nation with a unique form of government and with the unique opportunity to choose those who lead them. I believe they have the moral obligation to exercise that choice.

Nations matter. Citizenship matters. And as long as Christians in America (or any other country) have the ability to use their rights as citizens to effect the freedom of the gospel, the protection of liberty, or basic human flourishing, they should use it.

A Practical View

So, how can we best engage in ways that make a practical difference? Here are several ideas:

Pray for and encourage leaders: As we saw in Chapter 2, the most important thing we can do is to pray—for our country and for our leaders. First Timothy 2:1–2 specifically instructs us to do this: "I exhort therefore, that, first of all, supplications, prayers, intercessions, and giving of thanks, be made for all men; For kings, and for all that are in authority; that we may lead a quiet and peaceable life in all godliness and honesty."

But we can also directly reach out to those leaders serving as elected officials who are committed to standing for what is true and right. We need to encourage these leaders—pray for them, write them, thank them, and exercise our right to vote for them.

Vote: Although Jesus spoke primarily to our testimony and witness in reference to saying we are salt and light (Matthew 5:13–14), I believe this applies to any area in which we have influence. As Americans, we have a privilege not enjoyed by first-century Christians or, for that matter, Christians today in many other parts of the world—the opportunity to vote. I believe we should use that vote toward preserving our nation—including the freedoms that give us liberty to extend the light of the gospel.

Over the years, I have consistently cast my vote through a grid of three biblical issues: the sanctity of life (Jeremiah 1:5), the biblical family (Genesis 1:27, 2:24; Ephesians 5:22–25), and support for Israel (Genesis 12:3). I apply these qualifications to candidates on every level—federal, state, and county. I have rarely had the opportunity to vote for someone who thoroughly checked every box, and those candidates are becoming fewer. But I do my best to select based on who most closely stands to biblical positions on these issues.

Contact representatives on concerning issues: The fact that we elect our leaders makes it relevant to contact our leaders about concerning issues. Our representatives need to hear from us on the issues that matter to us. Many elected officials will respond to calls, letters, or emails from their constituents—especially when the response comes as a combined effort from multiple Christians.

Christians post online rants about ungodly legislation and the officials behind it. But they often fail to contact the officials directly. One phone call will go a long way. One letter will go even further.

Engage others: After you vote or call elected officials on urgent issues, seek to enlist those in your sphere of influence—neighbors, friends, co-workers, etc.—to also engage in these ways.

Serve in elected offices: From city councils to school boards, to national offices, we need Christians who are committed to America's founding values and to preserving religious liberty to serve in office. If God leads you to serve by running for these offices, do it. And don't discount running for local offices. A single vote on a school board or city council can make a huge difference.

Attend local meetings: Involve yourself in the betterment of your community. Attend city council and town hall meetings. Attend local school board meetings. (This is especially important for parents who have children in public schools. If you do not attend meetings, you don't know some of the egregious violations of parental rights and overt LGBTQ indoctrination that is being proposed.) Let your local leaders know that you are personally invested in making your community a better place.

Witness to local leaders: Our church family has done our best to develop positive relationships with our local leaders—our state representatives, city mayor, city council, law enforcement officers, and first responders. We host an annual appreciation day in their honor, and we create opportunities to show appreciation and share the gospel with them. I've had the opportunity to lead our city manager, congressmen, and others to Christ.

Sometimes when we look at the needs of our nation, particularly the ungodliness of some leaders and of the legislation being pushed, we can become so overwhelmed with a sense of hopelessness, that we do nothing. But when we remember Christ's statement that we are the "salt of the earth" and the "light of the world" (Matthew 5:13–14), we are encouraged that even one person can make a difference. A little salt flavors a lot of food. A little light shines in dark places.

Helen Keller had the right perspective when she said, "I am only one, but still I am one. I cannot do everything, but still I can do something; and because I cannot do everything, I will not refuse to do the something that I can do."[2]

There is much we cannot do, and we should trust God to work in ways we cannot. But that doesn't mean we can't do anything. What *can* you do? Do all you can.

A Heavenly View

Our first loyalty is not to America but to our King. Patriotic as we may be, we have an eternal homeland: "For our conversation is in heaven; from whence also we look for the Saviour, the Lord Jesus Christ: Who shall change our vile body, that it may be fashioned like unto his glorious body, according to the working whereby he is able even to subdue all things unto himself" (Philippians 3:20–21).

Like the Old Testament saints mentioned in Hebrews 11:13, we are "strangers and pilgrims on the earth." American Christians have the incredible privilege of being citizens of the freest nation in history on the face of this earth. But as long as we are on this earth, we're still strangers. You might say that we have dual citizenship—American and Heavenly.

As earthly citizens, it is our duty to engage in the betterment of our nation. As heavenly citizens, it is our duty to live with our affections and anticipation focused above. "For they that say such things declare plainly that they seek a country. And truly, if they had been mindful of that country from whence they came out, they might have had opportunity to have returned. But now they desire a better country, that is, an heavenly: wherefore God is not ashamed to be called their God: for he hath prepared for them a city" (Hebrews 11:14–16).

If my hope were in the United States of America, I would today be miserable indeed. But my hope is not in this country or in any other. My hope is in Jesus.

Yet, as a hope-filled citizen of Heaven, I am still a citizen of the United States. So I choose to remain informed and to engage in every way that I can while remembering that my greatest calling is to obey the Great Commission of Christ in sharing the gospel.

I do what I can, and I remember that while political movements come and go, while nations rise and fall, God remains on the throne. Whatever happens in the country I love does not control my destiny. Jesus does, and He has promised me a wonderful eternity.

So, yes, pray and vote and make phone calls. But do it all while keeping your eyes on your eternal homeland. This is what the righteous can—and should—do.

CONCLUSION

TRUST IN THE LORD

In the National Museum in Kraków, Poland, is an oil painting by Henry Siemiradzki titled "Nero's Torches." It depicts the gruesome scenes of men and women bound on high poles in Nero's gardens and being burned alive.

The painting is based on the accounts of first-century historians Tacitus and Suetonius, one of which we read in the introduction:

> In order to drown the rumor [that Nero had started the Great Fire of Rome], Nero fastened the guilt and inflicted the most exquisite tortures on a class…called Christians by the populace.…Covered with the skins of beasts, they were torn by dogs and perished, or were nailed to crosses, or were doomed to the flames and burnt, to serve as a nightly

> illumination, when daylight had expired. Nero offered his own gardens for this spectacle.[1]

There are many accounts of the persecution that first-century Christian endured. Nero's was the first government-organized persecution. Historians point to nine more crushing persecutions that followed. But even those ten provide an incomplete list. For even today Christians are being persecuted around the world—systemically persecuted in many countries.

So what did the Christians do?

Honestly, it's hard to find many individual records. I expect this is because it's hard to leave records when you are being hunted and slaughtered. But perhaps the most enduring record is the fact that we are talking about this today. Christians *continued.* In spite of the fiercest attacks against them, Christians passed on their faith from one generation to the next and from one geographic area to the next. They continued in the faith and shared the gospel.

What is a Christian to do? Keep practicing New Testament Christianity.

We began these pages with a question posed in Psalm 11 a thousand years before Nero's persecution of the

Christians: "If the foundations be destroyed, *what can the righteous do?*"

David, fleeing from King Saul and his maniacal quest to eliminate David, seems to have been asked this question of either in sarcasm or as a taunt. "Really, David, with Saul like he is and with the nation unraveling spiritually as it is, what *can* you do?"

I try to put myself in David's shoes. If I were a political outcast, constantly on the run from one wilderness asylum to the next, with the ever-present threat that my life would soon be taken, how would I have answered this fatalistic question?

It seems those who posed the question to David had a suggestion of their own: "Flee as a bird to your mountain" (Psalm 11:1). In other words, "David, it's hopeless. Give up, hide where you will never be hurt—and never be useful."

But David's answer was higher: "In the LORD put I my trust" (verse 1). And then in verses 4–7, David declared his trust in the sovereignty of God and God's goodness to reward the righteous.

> *The LORD is in his holy temple, the LORD's throne is in heaven: his eyes behold, his eyelids try, the children of men. The LORD trieth the righteous: but the wicked and him that loveth violence his soul hateth. Upon the*

> *wicked he shall rain snares, fire and brimstone, and an horrible tempest: this shall be the portion of their cup. For the righteous* Lord *loveth righteousness; his countenance doth behold the upright. (Psalm 11:4–7)*

We could summarize David's decision in this psalm, "I will trust God and keep doing right."

Living as a Bible-believing Christian today requires courage. What *is* a Christian who lives in a God-rejecting culture to do?

The answer is so simple that it's easy to miss: trust in the Lord.

Everything we have looked at in this book is helpful as far as it is an expression of our trust—*your* trust—in the Lord. On the other hand, if we are not trusting in the Lord as we engage in these activities, our efforts will be fruitless.

- We ***stand on truth*** because we trust God that His Word is true, righteous, preserved, and sufficient.
- We ***pray*** because we trust God to hear our prayers and intervene according to His will.

- We ***declare the gospel*** because we trust God's way of salvation and His ability to save even the most hardened souls.
- We ***commit to the local church*** because we trust God's design in forming the church as His body and we trust God to use it in our lives.
- We ***count the cost*** because we trust God to repay any sacrifice He calls us to make for His sake.
- We ***live with a consistent testimony*** because we trust that God is glorified through our lives and that our witness can draw others to Him.
- We ***teach the next generation*** because we trust God's promises to work through His Word in the hearts of children.
- We ***remain informed and engaged*** because we trust God to work through the nations He sets up and we believe He calls us to be proactive in a world that needs His light.

In every one of these areas, our trust is not ultimately in these activities. It is in the *Lord.* The earthy foundations of society have been destroyed and rebuilt again and again, but God's redemptive plan continues its victorious advance.

So *what* can the righteous do? They can trust in the Lord. And they can express that trust by practicing New Testament Christianity.

APPENDIX

WHO ARE THE RIGHTEOUS?

Righteous is a pretty big identifier to claim as your own. After all, none of us are perfect—or even close.

So what does "the righteous" mean in Psalm 11? And why would I write this book with the assumption that Bible-believing Christians are among "the righteous"?

Answering these questions is important to me for two reasons: First, I don't want you to read *righteous* and think I mean *self-righteous.* Second, I want you to know how *you* can be among the righteous.

No One Is Righteous

Before going any further, you need to know that God loves you. His love for you and me is based on the fact that He made us, not on our goodness—or lack of goodness. The most well-known verse in the Bible assures us that God loves every person.

> *For God so loved the world, that he gave his only begotten Son, that whosoever believeth in him should not perish, but have everlasting life. (John 3:16)*

But the Bible also tells us that we all fall short. Every last one of us are *un*righteous.

> *As it is written, There is none righteous, no, not one: (Romans 3:10)*

Have you ever wondered why, if God loves us, everyone in the world doesn't automatically have a relationship with Him? What is it that keeps us from God?

The Bible tells us that it is *sin* that separates us from God. Our sin creates an impassable chasm between us and God.

> *For all have sinned, and come short of the glory of God; (Romans 3:23)*

Sin is anything we do, say, or think that is against God's commandments. All of us sin, so all of us stand guilty before God. And we are separated from Him because of our sin.

In Romans 5:12 we see that ever since Adam and Eve (the first man and woman on earth) sinned, a sin nature has been present in all people. No one had to teach us how to sin; it comes naturally to us because none of us are born righteous.

> *Wherefore, as by one man sin entered into the world, and death by sin; and so death passed upon all men, for that all have sinned: (Romans 5:12)*

Self-Righteousness Is Not Enough

Some people believe that they can pay the price for sin by doing good works or being involved in religion. This may seem logical, but it's not what the Bible says. In fact, the Bible specifically tells us that we can't earn our way to Heaven through good works.

> *For by grace are ye saved through faith; and that not of yourselves: it is the gift of God: not of works, lest any man should boast. (Ephesians 2:8–9)*

The Bible does not tell us that the payment for our sin is good works; it tells us the payment is death.

> *For the wages of sin is death… (Romans 6:23)*

The "wage" or earned payment for our sin is spiritual death—eternal separation from God in Hell.

When we try to pay for our sins through good works, religion, sincerity, or any other effort, it won't work. In fact the Bible tells us that our efforts at righteousness are so tainted by our sin that they are like dirty rags.

> *But we are all as an unclean thing, and all our righteousnesses are as filthy rags; and we all do fade as a leaf; and our iniquities, like the wind, have taken us away. (Isaiah 64:6)*

No amount of good works can satisfy the payment that God set for sin.

A Gifted Righteousness

So, if we are not good enough on our own—if our own efforts at righteousness are not sufficient—how can we be righteous? Here is the answer: we cannot *earn* righteousness, but we can *receive* it.

Because God is love and He loves you, He made a way for you to have your sins forgiven. Jesus, who is God, came to this world, took on human flesh, and lived a perfect, sinless life. He then died on the cross—not for His sin (He never sinned), but to pay for our sin.

But God commendeth [demonstrated] his love toward us, in that, while we were yet sinners, Christ died for us. (Romans 5:8)

Think about how amazing this is: though we deserve eternal death for our sin, Jesus paid our debt when He died for our sin.

Jesus was buried and then rose from the dead three days later. He now offers us forgiveness and eternal life as a free gift.

For the wages of sin is death; but the gift of God is eternal life through Jesus Christ our Lord. (Romans 6:23)

A gift is not something we earn; it is simply something we receive.

You Can Be Reconciled to God through Christ

Although Jesus already paid for our sins and offers us a relationship with Him (and eternal life in Heaven too), we must choose to receive His gift. We must stop trusting ourselves, our works, and our religions, and place our full trust in Jesus Christ alone for the forgiveness of our sin.

How do we do this? The Bible tells us that we simply call out to Jesus to save us—to rescue us from the penalty of our sin.

For whosoever shall call upon the name of the Lord shall be saved. (Romans 10:13)

This is a promise directly from God that if you will confess to Him that you are a sinner, trust in the payment He made on the cross, and turn to Him alone to be your Savior, He will save you from the penalty of your sin. You can make that decision today by praying something like this from your heart:

Dear Lord, I know that I am separated from You because of sin. I confess that in my sin I cannot save myself. Right now, I turn to you alone to be my Saviour. I ask you to save me from the penalty of my sin, and I trust you to provide eternal life for me. Amen.

When you trust Christ as your personal Savior, the Bible tells us that the righteousness of Jesus now becomes your righteousness.

For he [God the Father] hath made him [God the Son] to be sin for us, who knew no sin; that we might be made the righteousness of God in him. (2 Corinthians 5:21)

That is real righteousness. It's not *earned* righteousness or *self*-righteousness. It is simply *received* righteousness.

If you just made the decision to stop trusting in yourself or your righteousness to earn a relationship with God and to receive the righteousness of Jesus, you just made the best decision of your life. He will never leave you or forsake you, and you are secure in your relationship with Him.

I hope you'll send an email to info@strivingtogether.com to let us know you made this decision. I would love to send you a Bible and resources to encourage your new life in Christ.

ENDNOTES

Introduction

1 Tacitus, *The Annals of Imperial Rome,* trans. Michael Grant (New York: Penguin Books, 1956), cited in Victor Duruy, *History of Rome,* vol. 5 (1883).

2 Tacitus, *Annals,* Book XV, Chapter 44, trans. Alfred John Church and William Jackson Brodribb (London: George Bell & Sons, 1905), cited in Victor Duruy, *History of Rome,* vol. 5 (1883).

3 Kristine Parks, "Christian 'Warrior' Speaks Out After Arrest for Reading Bible at Protest Against Drag Queen Performance for Kids," *Fox News,* June 16, 2023, https://www.foxnews.com/media/christian-warrior-speaks-arrest-reading-bible-protest-drag-queen-performance-kids.

4 Jessica Bates, "I'm a Christian and I'm Suing My State Because it Refused to Let Me Adopt Children," *Fox News,*

April 7, 2023, https://www.foxnews.com/opinion/ christian-suing-state-because-refused-letme-adopt-children.

5 Matt Snyder, "Dodgers Pride Night Timeline: Club Re-Invites Sisters of Perpetual Indulgence to LGBTQ+ Celebration," *CBS Sports,* June 17, 2023, https://www.cbssports.com/mlb/news/dodgers-pride-night-timeline-club-re-invites-sisters-of-perpetual-indulgence-to-lgbtq-celebration/.

6 Gavin Newsom, *Veto Message for AB 957,* September 30, 2023, https://www.gov.ca.gov/wp-content/uploads/2023/09/AB-957-Veto-Message.pdf.

Chapter 1

1 Benjamin Franklin, "Speech in the Constitutional Convention," June 28, 1787, in *The Records of the Federal Convention of 1787,* ed. Max Farrand (New Haven: Yale University Press, 1911), 92.

2 Benjamin Franklin, *Letter to George Whitefield,* September 17, 1757, in *The Works of Benjamin Franklin,* vol. 4, ed. John Bigelow (New York: G.P. Putnam's Sons, 1904), 438-440.

3 Donald Lutz, *The Origins of American Constitutionalism* (Baton Rouge, LA: LSU Press, 1988), 136–149

4 William Wilberforce, quoted in Ron Rhodes, *1001 Unforgettable Quotes About God, Faith, and the Bible* (Eugene, OR: Harvest House Publishers, 2011), 20.

Chapter 2

1 Rosalind Goforth, *How I Know God Answers Prayer* (Philadelphia, PA: The Sunday School Times Company, 1921), 15–16.

2 E. M. Bounds, *Power through Prayer* (Chicago, IL: Moody Press, 1979), 10.

Chapter 3

1 Winston S. Churchill, "We Shall Fight on the Beaches," speech delivered to the House of Commons, June 4, 1940, in *Churchill: A Life, by Martin Gilbert* (New York: Henry Holt and Company, 1991), 459.

2 R. Kent Hughes, *Colossians and Philemon: The Supremacy of Christ* (Westchester, IL: Crossway Books, 1989).

3 You might find my book, *Take It Personally* (Lancaster, CA: Striving Together Publications, 2016), helpful in learning how to lead someone to Christ.

Chapter 4

1 Romans, 1 and 2 Corinthians, Galatians, Ephesians, Philippians, Colossians, and 1 and 2 Thessalonians are all addressed to specific churches. First and 2 Timothy and Titus are addressed to local church leaders.

Chapter 5

1 John Lindsay, *The History of the Reformation in Scotland* (Edinburgh: William Blackwood and Sons, 1849), 154.

2 Carol Crawford Holcomb, "Commentary: Baptists and Religious Liberty—A Forgotten Story," *Baptist Standard,* September 19, 2023, https://www.baptiststandard.com/opinion/other-opinions/commentary-baptists-and-religious-liberty-a-forgotten-story/.

3 Minyvonne Burke, "Colorado Supreme Court to Hear Arguments in Transgender Cake Case," *NBC News,* June 19, 2024, https://www.nbcnews.com/nbc-out/out-news/colorado-supreme-court-hear-arguments-transgender-cake case-rcna157686.

4 Gary Fields, "High School Football Coach Who Got Job Back After Supreme Court Ruling Resigns," *AP News,* June 8, 2024, https://apnews.com/article/praying-high-school-football-coach-supreme-court-6a4bfa0f15771aa7ae4abeebe60d6c01.

5 Kristine Parks, "Pro-life activist facing up to 11 years in prison," *Fox News,* February 1, 2024, https://www.foxnews.com/media/pro-life-activist-facing-11-years-prison-peaceful-protest-makes-felon-bidens-doj.

6 Lindsay Kornick, "Twitter Erupts over Clip of UK Woman Arrested for Silently Praying Across from Abortion Clinic: 'Terrifying,'" *Fox News,* June 20, 2023, https://www.foxnews.com/media/twitter-erupts-clip-uk-woman-arrested-silently-praying-across-abortion-clinic-terrifying.

7 Samantha Kamman, "Christians faced record level of violent attacks in 2023, Open Doors warns," *The Christian Post,* January 17, 2024, https://www.christianpost.com/news/

christians-faced-record-level-of-violent-attacks-in-2023-report.html.

8 Oliver Burkeman, "Atheists, Agnostics and Non-Believers on the Meaning of Life," *The Guardian,* January 23, 2021, https://www.theguardian.com/global/2021/jan/23/atheists-agnostics-non-believers-on-the-meaning-of-life.

9 John Foxe, *Foxe's Book of Martyrs* (London: J. Barfield, 1843), 278-279.

Chapter 6

1 H. A. Ironside, *Illustrations of Bible Truth* (Chicago, IL: Moody Press, 1945), Kindle edition.

2 H. A. Ironside, *Except Ye Repent* (Chicago: Moody Press, 1930), 95.

Chapter 7

1 William L. Shirer, *The Rise and Fall of the Reich: A History of Nazi Germany* (Simon & Schuster, 2011), 249.

2 Los Angeles Unified School District, *Queer All School Year 2022-23* (Los Angeles: Los Angeles Unified School District, 2022), https://www.lausd.org/cms/lib/CA01000043/Centricity/domain/156/sogie/Queer%20All%20School%20Year%202223.pdf.

3 Alysia Gray Painter, "Tickets for Disneyland After Dark's Much-Anticipated Pride Nites Go on Sale," *NBC Los Angeles,* April 11, 2024, https://www.nbclosangeles.com/the-scene/

tickets-for-disneyland-after-darks-much-anticipated-pride-nites-go-on-sale/3384593/.

4 "Olivia Rodrigo Announces 'Plan B' Tour Tickets," *ABC7 Chicago,* March 14, 2024, https://abc7chicago.com/olivia-rodrigo-plan-b-tour-tickets/14524204/.

5 Philip Pullman, interview by Boyd Tonkin, "I Am of the Devil's Party," *The Telegraph,* February 17, 2002, https://www.telegraph.co.uk/culture/donotmigrate/3572490/I-am-of-the-Devils-party.html.

6 Philip Pullman, "The Shed Where God Died," *The Sydney Morning Herald,* December 13, 2003, https://www.smh.com.au/entertainment/books/the-shed-where-god-died-20031213-gdhz09.html.

Chapter 8

1 For a longer treatment of this time period and the one-world government, see Chapters 6–8 of my book *Understanding the Times* (Lancaster, CA: Striving Together Publications, 2021).

2 Forbes, "Quote by Helen Keller," *Forbes Quotes,* accessed August 1, 2024, https://www.forbes.com/quotes/3901/.

Conclusion

1 Tacitus, *Annals,* Book XV, Chapter 44, trans. Alfred John Church and William Jackson Brodribb (London: George Bell & Sons, 1905), cited in Victor Duruy, *History of Rome,* vol. 5 (1883).

ABOUT THE AUTHOR

DR. PAUL CHAPPELL is the senior pastor of Lancaster Baptist Church and president of West Coast Baptist College in Lancaster, California. He is a powerful communicator of God's Word and a passionate servant to God's people. He has been married to his wife, Terrie, since 1980, and they have four married children who are all serving in Christian ministry and eleven grandchildren. He enjoys spending time with his family and serving the Lord with a wonderful church family.

Dr. Chappell's preaching is heard on Daily in the Word, a radio program that is broadcast across America. You can find a station listing at paulchappell.com/radio.

You can connect with Dr. Chappell through his blog and social media:

paulchappell.com
x.com/paulchappell
instagram.com/paulchappell
facebook.com/pastor.paul.chappell

Other books by Paul Chappell . . .

ISBN: 978-1-59894-524-9

The fifty devotions in this book draw from the principles of God's Word that ignite our faith and deepen our courage in the Lord. Featuring ten different Bible characters and intertwining the stories of courageous Christians from the annals of history, these devotions will encourage and inspire you to courageously embrace God's call on your life and conquer obstacles in the power of His name.

STRIVINGTOGETHER.COM

ALSO AVAILABLE AS AN EBOOK